Sex Discrimination

Other Books in the Issues on Trial Series:

Sex Discrimination

Noël Merino, Book Editor

GREENHAVEN PRESS
A part of Gale, Cengage Learning

GALE
CENGAGE Learning·

Detroit • New York • San Francisco • New Haven, Conn • Waterville, Maine • London

Christine Nasso, *Publisher*
Elizabeth Des Chenes, *Managing Editor*

© 2010 Greenhaven Press, a part of Gale, Cengage Learning

For more information, contact:
Greenhaven Press
27500 Drake Rd.
Farmington Hills, MI 48331-3535
Or you can visit our Internet site at gale.cengage.com.

09-10

For product information and technology assistance, contact us at

Gale Customer Support, 1-800-877-4253
For permission to use material from this text or product, submit all requests online at
www.cengage.com/permissions

Further permissions questions can be emailed to permissionrequest@cengage.com

Articles in Greenhaven Press anthologies are often edited for length to meet page requirements. In addition, original titles of these works are changed to clearly present the main thesis and to explicitly indicate the author's opinion. Every effort is made to ensure that Greenhaven Press accurately reflects the original intent of the authors. Every effort has been made to trace the owners of copyrighted material.

Cover Image © Shawn Thew/epa/Corbis.

LIBRARY OF CONGRESS CATALOGING-IN-PUBLICATION DATA

Sex discrimination / Noël Merino, book editor.
p. cm. -- (Issues on trial)
Includes bibliographical references and index.
ISBN 978-0-7377-4740-9 (hardcover)
1. Sex discrimination--Law and legislation--United States--Cases--Juvenile literature. I. Merino, Noël.
KF4758.S487 2010
342.7308'7--dc22

2010000087

Printed in the United States of America
1 2 3 4 5 6 7 14 13 12 11 10

Contents

A retired U.S. Navy captain recounts the history of women in the U.S. military, noting the importance of several official actions that removed limitations to women's service, including the Court's decision in *Frontiero*.

Chapter 2: Striking Down Statutes Requiring Alimony Only of Men

Chapter 3: Upholding Affirmative Action for Working Women

Two attorneys contend that employers in the private sector are in a bind when it comes to ad hoc affirmative action, as the decision in *Johnson* seems to conflict with lower court decisions in later cases.

Chapter 4: Validating Limits on Suing Employers for Sex Discrimination

A legal policy analyst contends that the Lilly Ledbetter Fair Pay Act, overturning the decision in *Ledbetter*, is a bad idea and will harm the people it is intended to protect.

Foreword

The U.S. courts have long served as a battleground for the most highly charged and contentious issues of the time. Divisive matters are often brought into the legal system by activists who feel strongly for their cause and demand an official resolution. Indeed, subjects that give rise to intense emotions or involve closely held religious or moral beliefs lay at the heart of the most polemical court rulings in history. One such case was *Brown v. Board of Education* (1954), which ended racial segregation in schools. Prior to *Brown*, the courts had held that blacks could be forced to use separate facilities as long as these facilities were equal to that of whites.

For years many groups had opposed segregation based on religious, moral, and legal grounds. Educators produced heartfelt testimony that segregated schooling greatly disadvantaged black children. They noted that in comparison to whites, blacks received a substandard education in deplorable conditions. Religious leaders such as Martin Luther King Jr. preached that the harsh treatment of blacks was immoral and unjust. Many involved in civil rights law, such as Thurgood Marshall, called for equal protection of all people under the law, as their study of the Constitution had indicated that segregation was illegal and un-American. Whatever their motivation for ending the practice, and despite the threats they received from segregationists, these ardent activists remained unwavering in their cause.

Those fighting against the integration of schools were mainly white southerners who did not believe that whites and blacks should intermingle. Blacks were subordinate to whites, they maintained, and society had to resist any attempt to break down strict color lines. Some white southerners charged that segregated schooling was *not* hindering blacks' education. For example, Virginia attorney general J. Lindsay Almond asserted, "With the help and the sympathy and the love and re-spect of the white people of the South, the colored man has risen under that educational process to a place of eminence and respect throughout the nation. It has served him well." So when the Supreme Court ruled against the segregationists in *Brown*, the South responded with vociferous cries of protest. Even government leaders criticized the decision. The governor of Arkansas, Orval Faubus, stated that he would not "be a party to any attempt to force acceptance of change to which the people are so overwhelmingly opposed." Indeed, resistance to integration was so great that when black students arrived at the formerly all-white Central High School in Arkansas, federal troops had to be dispatched to quell a threatening mob of protesters.

Nevertheless, the *Brown* decision was enforced and the South integrated its schools. In this instance, the Court, while not settling the issue to everyone's satisfaction, functioned as an instrument of progress by forcing a major social change. Historian David Halberstam observes that the *Brown* ruling "deprived segregationist practices of their moral legitimacy. . . . It was therefore perhaps the single most important moment of the decade, the moment that separated the old order from the new and helped create the tumultuous era just arriving." Considered one of the most important victories for civil rights, *Brown* paved the way for challenges to racial segregation in many areas, including on public buses and in restaurants.

In examining *Brown*, it becomes apparent that the courts play an influential role—and face an arduous challenge—in shaping the debate over emotionally charged social issues. Judges must balance competing interests, keeping in mind the high stakes and intense emotions on both sides. As exemplified by *Brown*, judicial decisions often upset the status quo and initiate significant changes in society. Greenhaven Press's Issues on Trial series captures the controversy surrounding influential court rulings and explores the social ramifications of such decisions from varying perspectives. Each anthology highlights one social issue—such as the death penalty, students' rights, or wartime civil liberties. Each volume then focuses on key historical and contemporary court cases that helped mold the issue as we know it today. The books include a compendium of primary sources—court rulings, dissents, and immediate reactions to the rulings—as well as secondary sources from experts in the field, people involved in the cases, legal analysts, and other commentators opining on the implications and legacy of the chosen cases. An annotated table of contents, an in-depth introduction, and prefaces that overview each case all provide context as readers delve into the topic at hand. To help students fully probe the subject, each volume contains book and periodical bibliographies, a comprehensive index, and a list of organizations to contact. With these features, the Issues on Trial series offers a well-rounded perspective on the courts' role in framing society's thorniest, most impassioned debates.

Introduction

Sex discrimination refers to the different treatment of a person on the basis of sex. Both men and women can be the victims of sex discrimination, although historically it is women who have suffered the bulk of the negative effects of sex discrimination. The history of sex discrimination in the United States can be found in U.S. Supreme Court decisions, such as the 1873 case of *Bradwell v. Illinois*, wherein the Court upheld a law excluding women from practicing law, stating, "The natural and proper timidity and delicacy which belongs to the female sex evidently unfits it for many of the occupations of civil life."[1] A couple years later, in *Minor v. Happersett* (1875), the Court ruled that the U.S. Constitution did not grant women the right to vote. At the beginning of the twentieth century, in *Muller v. Oregon* (1908), the Court upheld Oregon's restrictions on the number of working hours of women due to their different physical structure, which allegedly could not handle the same demands of work as men.

The Nineteenth Amendment to the Constitution was ratified in 1920, giving women the right to vote: "The right of citizens of the United States to vote shall not be denied or abridged by the United States or by any State on account of sex." Beyond the Nineteenth Amendment, however, no provision of the Constitution explicitly prohibits sex discrimination.

Legal Redress for Sex Discrimination

Many federal laws have been enacted in the last several decades to prohibit sex discrimination, providing actionable legal redress for acts of sex discrimination. Two federal laws protect against sex discrimination in employment. The Equal Pay Act of 1963 requires that men and women must receive

1. *Bradwell v. Illinois*, U.S. Supreme Court, 1873.

equal pay for equal work in the same establishment, prohibiting sex discrimination in pay. Title VII of the Civil Rights Act of 1964 prohibits employment discrimination based on race, color, religion, sex, or national origin in regard to hiring, termination, promotion, compensation, job training, or any other condition of employment. The federal Fair Housing Act prohibits sex discrimination in the sale, rental, and financing of housing, while the Equal Credit Opportunity Act prohibits sex discrimination by creditors toward credit applicants. With respect to work and family, the Pregnancy Discrimination Act prohibits employment discrimination against female workers who are or intend to become pregnant, while the Family and Medical Leave Act gives employees (both men and women) the right to take time off from work to care for a newborn or an ill family member. Title IX of the Education Amendments of 1972 prohibits sex discrimination in education programs, including school athletic programs, that receive federal funds.

The parts of the Constitution that the Supreme Court has, since the 1970s, held to protect against sex discrimination are the equal protection and due process clauses of both the Fifth Amendment (which applies to the federal government) and the Fourteenth Amendment (which applies to the states). The equal protection clauses provide for equal protection of the law, whereas the due process clauses provide that a person not be deprived of "life, liberty, or property" without fair treatment under the law. Prior to the 1970s the courts had generally found that the biological differences between men and women justified different treatment under the law. Beginning with the Supreme Court decision in *Reed v. Reed* (1971), this began to change.

Sex Discrimination Cases in the Supreme Court

In *Reed*, a unanimous Supreme Court held that an Idaho statute preferring men to women in the administration of estates of the deceased violated the equal protection guaranteed by the Fourteenth Amendment. In the 1970s after *Reed,* numerous state and federal policies that treated men and women differently were invalidated by the Supreme Court, including federal law granting different family benefits for servicemen and servicewomen, in *Frontiero v. Richardson* (1973); state laws treating men and women differently with respect to drinking age, in *Craig v. Boren* (1976); federal law treating widows and widowers differently with respect to Social Security benefits, in *Califano v. Goldfarb* (1977); and state laws requiring alimony upon divorce from husbands but not wives, in *Orr v. Orr* (1979).

The cases that have come before the Supreme Court on the subject of sex discrimination involve a claim of different treatment due to one's sex. Men or women can make a charge of sex discrimination and in many cases where the Court has invalidated the different treatment of men and women, men have benefited from the termination of discriminatory treatment.

A notable exception to the Court's decisions mandating that men and women be treated the same is the Court's handling of affirmative action. Affirmative action with respect to sex involves taking account of a person's sex with respect to hiring decisions or school admission decisions in an attempt to promote equal opportunity and increase diversity. In *Johnson v. Transportation Agency* (1987), for instance, the Court determined that an employer's practice of using the sex of the employee to make a promotion decision in an attempt to remedy underrepresentation of women in the profession was not an instance of sex discrimination. Cases such as these are not without controversy, with many contending that any different treatment based on sex is always sex discrimination prohibited under the law.

Cases regarding sex discrimination continue to come before the Supreme Court, even when the issue at hand has presumably been settled. For instance, although it is a settled matter that it is sex discrimination to pay a woman differently than a man for the same work, there are limits on how much time a victim of sex discrimination has during which to bring a case to court. In *Ledbetter v. Goodyear Tire & Rubber Co.* (2007), the Supreme Court determined that the 180-day limit for filing sex discrimination claims regarding pay under Title VII of the Civil Rights Act was constitutional and dismissed Lilly Ledbetter's claim of sex discrimination. Congress is always able to pass legislation or a constitutional amendment if it disagrees with the Court's decisions, and it chose to do so in this instance. In 2009 the Lilly Ledbetter Fair Pay Act was enacted, allowing the 180-day limit to restart every time a person receives a discriminatory paycheck, even if a past discriminatory decision about pay was made long ago.

The Future of Sex Discrimination Cases

One of the issues that is likely to come before the Supreme Court in the future is that of how sex discrimination applies to transsexual individuals—biological men who later become women and biological women who later become men. Recently a federal district court, in *Schroer v. Billington* (2008), determined that a transsexual denied employment based on her transsexuality was the victim of sex discrimination. In this instance sex discrimination applied to an action taken by an employer based on the chosen sex of the individual rather than the biological sex.

This anthology seeks to explore the debate about sex discrimination by looking at four major U.S. Supreme Court decisions related to sex discrimination in America: *Frontiero v. Richardson* (1973), *Orr v. Orr* (1979), *Johnson v. Transportation Agency* (1987), and *Ledbetter v. Goodyear Tire & Rubber Co.* (2007). By presenting the Supreme Court's decisions, the views of dissenting justices, and commentary on the impact of the cases, *Issues on Trial: Sex Discrimination* sheds light on how the legal understanding of sex discrimination in the United States has evolved and continues to evolve.

CHAPTER 1

Sex Discrimination in Military Benefits

Case Overview

Frontiero v. Richardson (1973)

In *Frontiero v. Richardson* the U.S. Supreme Court considered the constitutionality of federal statutes that provided members of the armed services with certain spousal benefits, with limitations on what servicewomen could receive as compared to servicemen. Eight of the justices agreed that the statutes' different treatment on the basis of sex violated the due process clause of the Fifth Amendment, with one justice dissenting.

Sharron Frontiero was a lieutenant in the United States Air Force, and her husband was a full-time student in Montgomery, Alabama. They challenged the constitutionality of federal statutes that provided benefits for the dependents of service personnel, allowing married servicemen to receive an automatic increase in these benefits for a dependent spouse while requiring a married servicewoman to prove the dependency of her spouse in order to receive increased benefits. The Frontieros argued that different treatment for female members of the armed forces under these statutes constituted unconstitutional sex discrimination. The U.S. government conceded that the differential treatment on the basis of sex served no other purpose than administrative convenience, because wives were more frequently dependent upon husbands whereas husbands were rarely dependent upon their wives, making it cheaper and easier to presume the dependency of the wives of servicemen, while making servicewomen prove their husband's dependency.

The case was first brought to the district court, which found that the statutes in question were constitutional. The Frontieros then appealed to the Supreme Court, which reversed the district court's ruling. The Court found that the statutes were in violation of the due process clause of the

Fifth Amendment, constituting sex discrimination by requiring women to prove the dependency of their spouses in order to get increased benefits while not requiring any such proof from men.

The Court's decision in this case constituted a plurality rather than a majority, given that while the eight justices agreed that the statues were unconstitutional, they disagreed (with four justices on each side) about the reasoning used to establish this unconstitutionality. The central disagreement among the justices was what level of scrutiny the Court ought to use in reviewing statutes that draw distinctions based on sex: Half the justices in the plurality believed that such statutes should get the highest level of review—strict scrutiny— whereas the other half thought that the Court should be more deferential to the legislature and only review such statutes with intermediate scrutiny. Regardless of this difference, the case was notable in that all eight justices in the plurality agreed that some level of heightened scrutiny above the usual deferential review was needed for laws that involved different treatment on the basis of sex, due to the history of sex discrimination. The exception was Justice William Rehnquist, who made a short dissenting statement opining that the statutes were constitutional under the lowest standard of review.

This key disagreement between the two sides in the plurality was resolved a few years later in *Craig v. Boren* (1976), wherein the Court determined that sex-based classifications in laws and regulations deserved an intermediate level of scrutiny, a practice that continues today. Whereas laws and regulations that make classifications based on race always are reviewed in the strictest manner, classifications based on sex are seen as being less egregious and so have a slightly lower standard of review by the Court. The debate among the justices about this issue makes it of historical importance.

> "Classifications based upon sex, like clas-
> sifications based upon race, alienage, or
> national origin, are inherently suspect,
> and must therefore be subjected to strict
> judicial scrutiny."

The Court's Decision: Differential Treatment of Men and Women Is Unconstitutional

William J. Brennan Jr.

William J. Brennan Jr. was a justice of the U.S. Supreme Court from 1956 to 1990. He is best known for his liberal views oppos-ing the death penalty and supporting abortion rights.

The following is the plurality opinion in the 1973 case of Frontiero v. Richardson, *in which four members of the Supreme Court joined in full and another four justices joined in part, with all agreeing to the unconstitutionality of the statute. This ruling reversed the district court ruling that upheld a law allow-ing male servicemen to claim their wives as dependents without any proof of dependency for the purpose of receiving benefits, while requiring female servicewomen to prove dependency of their husbands in order to receive similar benefits. Writing for the Court, Justice Brennan found that such a statute violates the due process clause of the Fifth Amendment by treating male and female service members differently with respect to proof of de-pendency.*

William J. Brennan Jr., plurality opinion, *Frontiero v. Richardson*, U.S. Supreme Court, 1973.

The question before us concerns the right of a female member of the uniformed services to claim her spouse as a "dependent" for the purposes of obtaining increased quarters allowances and medical and dental benefits under 37 U.S.C. §§ 401 403, and 10 U.S.C. §§ 1072 1076, on an equal footing with male members. Under these statutes, a serviceman may claim his wife as a "dependent" without regard to whether she is in fact, dependent upon him for any part of her support. A servicewoman, on the other hand, may not claim her husband as a "dependent" under these programs unless he is in fact, dependent upon her for over one-half of his support. Thus, the question for decision is whether this difference in treatment constitutes an unconstitutional discrimination against servicewomen in violation of the Due Process Clause of the Fifth Amendment. A three-judge District Court for the Middle District of Alabama, one judge dissenting, rejected this contention and sustained the constitutionality of the provisions of the statutes making this distinction. We noted probable jurisdiction. We reverse.

Fringe Benefits for Service Members

In an effort to attract career personnel through reenlistment, Congress established a scheme for the provision of fringe benefits to members of the uniformed services on a competitive basis with business and industry. Thus, under 37 U.S.C. § 403 a member of the uniformed services with dependents is entitled to an increased "basic allowance for quarters" and, under 10 U.S.C. § 1076 a member's dependents are provided comprehensive medical and dental care.

Appellant Sharron Frontiero, a lieutenant in the United States Air Force, sought increased quarters allowances, and housing and medical benefits for her husband, appellant Joseph Frontiero, on the ground that he was her "dependent." Although such benefits would automatically have been granted with respect to the wife of a male member of the uniformed services, appellant's application was denied because she failed to demonstrate that her husband was dependent on her for more than one-half of his support. Appellants then commenced this suit, contending that, by making this distinction, the statutes unreasonably discriminate on the basis of sex in violation of the Due Process Clause of the Fifth Amendment. In essence, appellants asserted that the discriminatory impact of the statutes is twofold: first, as a procedural matter, a female member is required to demonstrate her spouse's dependency, while no such burden is imposed upon male members; and, second, as a substantive matter, a male member who does not provide more than one-half of his wife's support receives benefits, while a similarly situated female member is denied such benefits. Appellants therefore sought a permanent injunction against the continued enforcement of these statutes and an order directing the appellees to provide Lieutenant Frontiero with the same housing and medical benefits that a similarly situated male member would receive.

The District Court Decision

Although the legislative history of these statutes sheds virtually no light on the purposes underlying the differential treatment accorded male and female members, a majority of the three-judge District Court surmised that Congress might reasonably have concluded that, since the husband in our society is generally the "breadwinner" in the family—and the wife typically the "dependent" partner—

> it would be more economical to require married female members claiming husbands to prove actual dependency than to extend the presumption of dependency to such members.

Indeed, given the fact that approximately 99% of all members of the uniformed services are male, the District Court speculated that such differential treatment might conceivably lead to a "considerable saving of administrative expense and manpower."

Court Review of Sex-Based Classifications

At the outset, appellants contend that classifications based upon sex, like classifications based upon race, alienage, and national origin, are inherently suspect, and must therefore be subjected to close judicial scrutiny. We agree, and, indeed, find at least implicit support for such an approach in our unanimous decision only last Term in *Reed v. Reed* (1971).

In *Reed*, the Court considered the constitutionality of an Idaho statute providing that, when two individuals are otherwise equally entitled to appointment as administrator of an estate, the male applicant must be preferred to the female. Appellant, the mother of the deceased, and appellee, the father, filed competing petitions for appointment as administrator of their son's estate. Since the parties, as parents of the deceased, were members of the same entitlement class, the statutory preference was invoked, and the father's petition was therefore granted. Appellant claimed that this statute, by giving a mandatory preference to males over females without regard to their individual qualifications, violated the Equal Protection Clause of the Fourteenth Amendment.

The Court noted that the Idaho statute

> provides that different treatment be accorded to the applicants on the basis of their sex; it thus establishes a classification subject to scrutiny under the Equal Protection Clause.

Under "traditional" equal protection analysis, a legislative classification must be sustained unless it is "patently arbitrary" and bears no rational relationship to a legitimate governmental interest.

In an effort to meet this standard, appellee contended that the statutory scheme was a reasonable measure designed to reduce the workload on probate courts by eliminating one class of contests. Moreover, appellee argued that the mandatory preference for male applicants was, in itself, reasonable, since "men [are], as a rule, more conversant with business affairs than . . . women." Indeed, appellee maintained that

> it is a matter of common knowledge that women still are not engaged in politics, the professions, business or industry to the extent that men are.

And the Idaho Supreme Court, in upholding the constitutionality of this statute, suggested that the Idaho Legislature might reasonably have "concluded that, in general, men are better qualified to act as an administrator than are women."

Despite these contentions, however, the Court held the statutory preference for male applicants unconstitutional. In reaching this result, the Court implicitly rejected appellee's apparently rational explanation of the statutory scheme, and concluded that, by ignoring the individual qualifications of particular applicants, the challenged statute provided "dissimilar treatment for men and women who are . . . similarly situated." The Court therefore held that, even though the State's interest in achieving administrative efficiency "is not without some legitimacy,"

> [t]o give a mandatory preference to members of either sex over members of the other merely to accomplish the elimination of hearings on the merits is to make the very kind of arbitrary legislative choice forbidden by the [Constitution]. . . .

This departure from "traditional" rational basis analysis with respect to sex-based classifications is clearly justified.

A History of Sex Discrimination

There can be no doubt that our Nation has had a long and unfortunate history of sex discrimination. Traditionally, such discrimination was rationalized by an attitude of "romantic paternalism" which, in practical effect, put women not on a pedestal, but in a cage. Indeed, this paternalistic attitude became so firmly rooted in our national consciousness that, 100 years ago, a distinguished Member of this Court was able to proclaim:

> Man is, or should be, woman's protector and defender. The natural and proper timidity and delicacy which belongs to the female sex evidently unfits it for many of the occupations of civil life. The constitution of the family organization, which is founded in the divine ordinance as well as in the nature of things, indicates the domestic sphere as that which properly belongs to the domain and functions of womanhood. The harmony, not to say identity, of interests and views which belong, or should belong, to the family institution is repugnant to the idea of a woman adopting a distinct and independent career from that of her husband. . . .
>
> . . . The paramount destiny and mission of woman are to fulfil the noble and benign offices of wife and mother. This is the law of the Creator [*Bradwell v. State* (1873)].

As a result of notions such as these, our statute books gradually became laden with gross, stereotyped distinctions between the sexes, and, indeed, throughout much of the 19th century, the position of women in our society was, in many respects, comparable to that of blacks under the pre-Civil War slave codes. Neither slaves nor women could hold office, serve on juries, or bring suit in their own names, and married women traditionally were denied the legal capacity to hold or convey property or to serve as legal guardians of their own children. And although blacks were guaranteed the right to vote in 1870, women were denied even that right—which is itself "preservative of other basic civil and political rights"— until adoption of the Nineteenth Amendment half a century later.

It is true, of course, that the position of women in America has improved markedly in recent decades. Nevertheless, it can hardly be doubted that, in part because of the high visibility of the sex characteristic, women still face pervasive, although at times more subtle, discrimination in our educational institutions, in the job market and, perhaps most conspicuously, in the political arena.

The Problem with Sex-Based Classifications

Moreover, since sex, like race and national origin, is an immutable characteristic determined solely by the accident of birth, the imposition of special disabilities upon the members of a particular sex because of their sex would seem to violate "the basic concept of our system that legal burdens should bear some relationship to individual responsibility. . . ." [*Weber v. Aetna Casualty & Surety Co.* (1972)]. And what differentiates sex from such nonsuspect statuses as intelligence or physical disability, and aligns it with the recognized suspect criteria, is that the sex characteristic frequently bears no relation to ability to perform or contribute to society. As a result, statutory distinctions between the sexes often have the effect of invidiously relegating the entire class of females to inferior legal status without regard to the actual capabilities of its individual members.

We might also note that, over the past decade, Congress has itself manifested an increasing sensitivity to sex-based classifications. In Tit. VII of the Civil Rights Act of 1964, for example, Congress expressly declared that no employer, labor union, or other organization subject to the provisions of the Act shall discriminate against any individual on the basis of "race, color, religion, *sex*, or national origin." Similarly, the Equal Pay Act of 1963 provides that no employer covered by the Act "shall discriminate . . . between employees on the basis of *sex*." And § 1 of the Equal Rights Amendment, passed by Congress on March 22, 1972, and submitted to the legislatures of the States for ratification, declares that "[e]quality of rights under the law shall not be denied or abridged by the United States or by any State on account of sex." Thus, Congress itself has concluded that classifications based upon sex are inherently invidious, and this conclusion of a coequal branch of Government is not without significance to the question presently under consideration.

With these considerations in mind, we can only conclude that classifications based upon sex, like classifications based upon race, alienage, or national origin, are inherently suspect, and must therefore be subjected to strict judicial scrutiny. Applying the analysis mandated by that stricter standard of review, it is clear that the statutory scheme now before us is constitutionally invalid.

The Justification for Differential Treatment

The sole basis of the classification established in the challenged statutes is the sex of the individuals involved. Thus, under 37 U.S.C. §§ 401 403, and 10 U.S.C. §§ 1072 1076, a female member of the uniformed services seeking to obtain housing and medical benefits for her spouse must prove his dependency in fact, whereas no such burden is imposed upon male members. In addition, the statutes operate so as to deny benefits to a female member, such as appellant Sharron Frontiero, who provides less than one-half of her spouse's support, while at the same time granting such benefits to a male member who likewise provides less than one-half of his spouse's support. Thus, to this extent, at least, it may fairly be said that these statutes command "dissimilar treatment for men and women who are . . . similarly situated" [*Reed v. Reed*].

Moreover, the Government concedes that the differential treatment accorded men and women under these statutes serves no purpose other than mere "administrative convenience." In essence, the Government maintains that, as an empirical matter, wives in our society frequently are dependent upon their husbands, while husbands rarely are dependent upon their wives. Thus, the Government argues that Congress might reasonably have concluded that it would be both cheaper and easier simply conclusively to presume that wives of male members are financially dependent upon their husbands, while burdening female members with the task of establishing dependency in fact.

A Higher Value than Convenience

The Government offers no concrete evidence, however, tending to support its view that such differential treatment in fact saves the Government any money. In order to satisfy the demands of strict judicial scrutiny, the Government must demonstrate, for example, that it is actually cheaper to grant increased benefits with respect to all male members than it is to determine which male members are, in fact, entitled to such benefits, and to grant increased benefits only to those members whose wives actually meet the dependency requirement. Here, however, there is substantial evidence that, if put to the test, many of the wives of male members would fail to qualify for benefits. And in light of the fact that the dependency determination with respect to the husbands of female members is presently made solely on the basis of affidavits, rather than through the more costly hearing process, the Government's explanation of the statutory scheme is, to say the least, questionable.

In any case, our prior decisions make clear that, although efficacious administration of governmental programs is not without some importance, "the Constitution recognizes higher values than speed and efficiency" [*Stanley v. Illinois* (1972)]. And when we enter the realm of "strict judicial scrutiny," there can be no doubt that "administrative convenience" is not a shibboleth [something that distinguishes people of one group from another], the mere recitation of which dictates constitutionality. On the contrary, any statutory scheme which draws a sharp line between the sexes, solely for the purpose of achieving administrative convenience, necessarily commands "dissimilar treatment for men and women who are ... similarly situated," and therefore involves the "very kind of arbitrary legislative choice forbidden by the [Constitution]. . . ." [*Reed v. Reed*]. We therefore conclude that, by according differential treatment to male and female members of the uniformed services for the sole purpose of achieving administrative convenience, the challenged statutes violate the Due Process Clause of the Fifth Amendment insofar as they require a female member to prove the dependency of her husband.

> *"The housing and medical benefits statutes here challenged do not violate the due process clause of the Fifth Amendment."*

The Statute in Question Treating Men and Women Differently Is Reasonable

Erwin N. Griswold, Harlington Wood Jr., Mark L. Evans, et al.

Erwin N. Griswold was U.S. solicitor general, Harlington Wood Jr. was assistant attorney general for the U.S. Department of Justice, and Mark L. Evans was assistant to the solicitor general representing U.S. Secretary of Defense Elliot L. Richardson and the other U.S. government appellees in Frontiero v. Richardson *(1973).*

In the following excerpt from the brief submitted for the U.S. government, the attorneys argue that the benefits statutes in question in Frontiero *that treat male and female service members differently are not unconstitutional. The attorneys contend that the justification for the differential treatment of the servicemen and servicewomen with respect to proving dependency is reasonable. Furthermore, they argue that it is improper for the Court to consider sex a suspect classification, which would require a compelling interest instead of a rational basis for the law.*

The standard for review of legislative classifications in the area of economic benefits is whether the classification is reasonably related to a proper legislative objective. Under this

Erwin N. Griswold, Harlington Wood Jr., Mark L. Evans, et al., brief for the appellees, *Frontiero v. Richardson*, U.S. Supreme Court, 1973.

test the housing and medical benefits statutes here challenged do not violate the due process clause of the Fifth Amendment. The objective of the statutes is to provide benefits for dependents of members of the uniformed services. The Congress could reasonably conclude that the economical administration of the dependency benefits program would be better served by not requiring an individual examination of each claim for benefits by the nearly one and one-half million married male members of the services, in view of the likelihood that the wives of most members are in fact dependent on their husbands. By the same token, the Congress could reasonably determine that, since there are only some 4,000 married female members and since it is likely that their husbands are not dependent upon them, the purposes of the dependency benefits program would be best served by granting benefits only to those whose husbands are in fact dependent.

This Court's recent decision in *Reed v. Reed* [1971], striking down a state statutory preference for men as administrators of estates, is distinguishable from this case. In *Reed*, the State had sought to implement a legitimate objective—"reducing the workload on probate courts by eliminating one class of contests"—by arbitrarily preferring men over women when there was no reason to think that men would perform better than women. Here, however, the presumptions of dependency are reasonably related to the legislative purpose and to the economic realities of our society.

Appellant's contention that the statutory classifications must be struck down because they reflect a "sex stereotype" that is no longer acceptable should, we submit, be addressed to the Congress, not the courts, for the challenge concerns the wisdom, not the reasonableness, of the legislative choice. . . .

Sex Classifications

Although the classifications have a rational basis and are therefore constitutional under the traditional test, appellants argue that the standard for reviewing sex classifications should be the same as that applied for race, national origin, and alienage: whether the classification is necessary to the accomplishment of compelling governmental interests. Sex, however, does not share most of the qualities that have led to the rigid scrutiny of classifications based on race, nationality, or alienage. Sex classifications do not have the especially disfavored constitutional status of race classifications; they do not affect a "discrete and insular" minority which has been excluded from the political process; they neither stigmatize nor imply a legislative judgment of female inferiority; and they are not, like race or nationality, presumptively arbitrary.

Sex classifications are, therefore, not "inherently suspect" under the Fifth Amendment. If, as appellants urge, they are frequently unwise as a matter of national policy, then the proper remedy is by legislation or constitutional amendment, rather than by abrupt judicial departure from familiar constitutional principles. We accordingly think it significant that, apart from the recent legislative activity with respect to the statutes in issue here, the Congress has approved, and 22 states have ratified, the Equal Rights Amendment to the Constitution [it never received the 38 state ratifications necessary to pass].

A Reasonable Statute

While the Fifth Amendment has no equal protection clause, it forbids discrimination that is "so unjustifiable as to be violative of due process" [*Bolling v. Sharpe* (1954)]. In statutes dealing with economic benefits, a legislative classification must be upheld "'if any state of facts reasonably may be conceived to justify it'" [*Dandridge v. Williams* (1970)]. Such a classification is constitutionally infirm only if it is "patently arbitrary" and bears no rational relationship to the objective sought to be advanced by the statute [*Flemming v. Nestor* (1960)].

Under these criteria, the statutes involved here are constitutional. As the court below stated, the legislative objective of the dependents' living allowance and medical benefits provisions is to reimburse members for the expense of furnishing shelter to their dependents and to provide free medical care for their dependents. The challenged classification reasonably implements these goals and the legitimate interest of Congress in the effective administration of the dependency benefits program.

The legislative history of the statutes sheds little light on the reasons for the different treatment of male and female members of the service. The legislative plan, which extends automatic dependency benefits only to male members of the service, obviously reflects the congressional judgment that most wives are dependent upon their husbands. In view of the large number of married male members of the armed forces and the likelihood that most of their wives are dependent upon them, Congress could properly determine that it would be an unnecessary burden on the dependency benefits program to require that each application for benefits be examined and investigated. It was therefore justified in concluding that the statutory objectives would best be served by granting benefits to all married male personnel, notwithstanding that a small proportion of servicemen whose wives are not dependent would receive a windfall in the form of unneeded benefits.

In the case of female married members of the uniformed services, it was not unreasonable for Congress to have concluded that most of their husbands are not dependent and that the federal interest in economical administration of the program would therefore be promoted by examining individually the much smaller number of claims involved. Thus, while female members whose husbands are in fact dependent on them are entitled to benefits, the relatively large percentage whose husbands are not dependent receive no windfall.

The Difference with *Reed*

It is the reasonableness of the classification that distinguishes this case from *Reed v. Reed*, upon which appellants rely. In *Reed*, this Court struck down, as violative of the Fourteenth Amendment's equal protection clause, Idaho's statutory preference for men as administrators of estates. The State sought to justify the preference on the ground that the time and effort involved in selecting administrators could be reduced by eliminating the need to consider women for the position. The Court recognized that "the objective of reducing the workload on probate courts by eliminating one class of contests is not without some legitimacy." It held however, that the means chosen to achieve that objective were arbitrary. Since men and women are equally capable of performing the duties of an administrator, the statute sought to reduce administrative costs by establishing a classification without a rational basis.

Here, by contrast, the classification chosen by Congress to achieve administrative economies is based upon reasonable presumptions of dependency, which are in accord with the realities of American life. The statute therefore does not infringe the Fifth Amendment rights of female members of the armed forces, and *Reed* does not require that it be declared unconstitutional. . . .

The Right Standard of Review

As the foregoing discussion demonstrates, the classification here bears a reasonable relationship to the objectives of the legislation. Under traditional equal protection principles, therefore, the statutes do not offend the Fifth Amendment's due process clause. Appellants argue, however, that legislative classifications relating in any way to sex—with the exception of those which are "protective," "remedial," or "neutral"—can be sustained only if necessary to the accomplishment of compelling governmental interests.

This strict standard of review, however, has been limited to classifications that either affect sensitive and fundamental personal rights or are inherently suspect. We do not understand appellants to argue that the interests here at issue—which are wholly economic—qualify as fundamental rights. This Court has held that when, as here, the government operates in the area of economics and social welfare, legislative classifications must be sustained if they have a reasonable basis, even though they be "imperfect" or may in practice result in some inequality.

Appellants do contend that sex—like race, national origin, and alienage—must be viewed as a "suspect" basis for classification and therefore must satisfy the stricter "compelling interest" test. This Court, however, has never treated classifications based on sex as inherently suspect, and we do not think appellants have borne their heavy burden of showing that it has become necessary to review sex classifications under the compelling interest standard.

Sex and Suspect Classifications

It is true that sex, like race and national origin, is a visible and immutable biological characteristic that bears no necessary relation to ability. But sex does not share most of the other qualities that have led the Court to give rigid scrutiny to legislative classifications based on race, nationality, or alienage. First, racial distinctions, unlike sex distinctions, have an especially disfavored status in constitutional history; they "must be viewed in light of the historical fact that the central purpose of the Fourteenth Amendment was to eliminate racial discrimination emanating from official sources in the States" [*McLaughlin v. Florida* (1964)]. It is this "strong policy [that] renders racial classifications 'constitutionally suspect.'"

Suspect classifications have, moreover, invariably affected disadvantaged minorities, which, because of their minority status, have been especially vulnerable to the attempts of more powerful—and often hostile—political forces seeking to deprive them of equal rights. "[P]rejudice against discrete and insular minorities" thus calls for a more searching judicial inquiry because of the likely unresponsiveness of "those political processes ordinarily to be relied upon to protect minorities" [*United States v. Carolene Products Co.* (1938)]. Women, of course, are a numerical majority in this country and surely are not disabled from exerting their substantial and growing political influence. Even the female members of the uniformed services, though only a small minority, are not "discrete" in the sense that ethnic minorities are discrete, and are plainly not "insular." Nor is there any indication that the political process has excluded or ignored them. Indeed, if the recent bills to amend the dependency benefits statutes are any indication, this minority has a potent political voice.

Nor is legislation affecting women, like that affecting racial or ethnic minorities, commonly perceived as implying a stigma of inferiority or a badge of opprobrium which suggests that the affected class lacks equal dignity. In *Strauder v. West Virginia* [1879], this Court held that a state statute precluding blacks from serving on juries "is practically a brand upon them . . . an assertion of their inferiority, and a stimulant to . . . race prejudice. . . ." The Fourteenth Amendment, the Court stated, prohibits "legal discriminations, implying inferiority in civil society." It is, we submit, for similar reasons that classifications based on nationality and alienage, as well as those based on race, are subjected to close scrutiny.

Classifications based on sex, however, do not express an implied legislative judgment of female inferiority. Sex classifications are commonly founded upon physiological and sociological differences, and not on social contempt for women. Statutes which, for example, limit the employment of women as bartenders, or exempt women from the draft, bear no connotation of female inferiority, but rather are properly regarded as based upon objective differences between the sexes. Thus, sex classifications are no more likely to stigmatize than legislation affecting any other identifiable group, such as the elderly, veterans, or the unemployed.

The Relevance of Sex Differences

The decisions of this Court suggest also that a legislative classification is inherently suspect only when it is, in effect, presumptively arbitrary. Thus, legislation imposing an unequal burden upon ethnic groups or racial minorities is immediately suspect because racial and ethnic characteristics are, except in the most extraordinary circumstances, irrelevant to any proper legislative purpose. Accordingly, a classification drawn in these terms fairly raises a presumption that the object sought to be attained by the statutory distinction is constitutionally impermissible, or that the means chosen are unrelated to a legitimate objective.

Such a presumption of invalidity, however, is inappropriate in the case of classifications based upon sex, for that characteristic frequently bears a reasonable relation to a legitimate governmental purpose. This Court has sustained legislative classifications predicated upon the sociological or physiological differences between the sexes, when these differences are relevant to such purpose. Thus, the Court has upheld statutes permitting a state university to provide separate branches for male and female students; relieving women of jury duty unless they volunteered, thereby permitting women to determine whether jury service would be consistent with their family responsibilities; and limiting working hours of women on the basis of medical evidence of the injurious effect of long working hours upon a woman's constitution. By the same token, where sex differences are manifestly irrelevant to the particular objective sought to be attained by the legislature, this Court has found the classification constitutionally invalid.

We therefore submit that the Fifth Amendment does not require application of the compelling interest test to sex classifications.

| *"The achievement of social equality for women has been a long journey."*

The Decision in *Frontiero* Was a Key Step Toward Equality for Women

Christine Basic

Christine Basic is a deputy public defender in California.

In the following article Basic argues that the decision in Frontiero v. Richardson *(1973) was one of the first and most important steps toward the achievement of social equality for women. She notes that although the eight justices who voted for the unconstitutionality of the statute that treated male and female service members differently disagreed in their justification, they did all agree that such a law could not stand up to Court review. Basic celebrates the fact that since* Frontiero, *in spite of the fact that the classification of sex has not been embraced as wholly suspect in the same way as race, it has gotten much closer and states do have to offer substantial justification for any laws that treat men and women differently.*

Often denied the same opportunities and privileges freely accessible to their male counterparts, women have stood on the outside looking through the proverbial glass window for most of recorded history. In recognizing that gender "frequently bears no relation to ability to perform or contribute to society," the Court in *Frontiero v. Richardson* [1973] takes the first step toward a constitutional remedy for the second-class citizenship of this nation's wives.

Christine Basic, "Strict Scrutiny and the Sexual Revolution: *Frontiero v. Richardson*," *Journal of Contemporary Legal Issues*, vol. 14, no. 1, Summer 2004, pp. 117–29. Copyright © 2004 Journal of Contemporary Legal Issues. Reproduced by permission.

The Frontieros' Case in District Court

In 1970 Lieutenant Sharron Frontiero USAF applied for the housing and medical benefits offered to members of the U.S. military who had dependents in their households. She claimed her husband, a full-time college student, as a dependent. The statutory benefits scheme, however, openly discriminated between similarly situated male and female service members. Unlike her male military colleagues, who only had to prove they were married to be entitled to these household allowances, Sharron also had to prove that her husband was dependent on her for more than half of his support.

Sharron and her husband challenged this federal entitlements scheme as a violation of the Fifth Amendment's Due Process Clause. A three-judge federal district court denied their demand for declaratory and injunctive relief. Treating the statutory scheme as involving matters of "economics and social welfare," that court decided it must be upheld "if any state of facts rationally justifying it is demonstrated or perceived by the courts." Few married women were in the military service, the district court guessed; and fewer still were their families' primary breadwinners. The court discovered a rational justification in administrative convenience:

> It seems clear that the reason Congress established a conclusive presumption in favor of married service men was to avoid imposing on the uniformed services a substantial administrative burden of requiring actual proof from some 200,000 male officers and over 1,000,000 enlisted men that their wives were actually dependent upon them.... Congress apparently reached the conclusion that it would be more economical to require married female members claiming husbands to prove actual dependency than to extend the presumption of dependency to such members.... In other words, the alleged injustice of the distinction lies in the possibility that some married service men are getting "windfall" payments, while married service women are denied them.

The United States Supreme Court accepted the Frontieros' appeal, and reversed.

Common Ends, Fractured Means

Eight Justices agreed that the federal statutes in *Frontiero* unconstitutionally discriminated between men and women, but they split evenly on the standards leading to their conclusion. Eight Justices rested their analysis of the statutes' unconstitutionality on a single recent precedent, but again split evenly over what that precedent meant.

Many consider *Reed v. Reed* [1971], decided just two terms before *Frontiero*, to be the progenitor of the Supreme Court's modern gender-discrimination jurisprudence. In *Reed*, a unanimous Court declared an Idaho probate scheme, which required that males be preferred over females when equally situated (for example, as children, parents, siblings) in contests for administration of an intestate estate, to violate the Equal Protection Clause. The *Reed* Court rejected as insufficient the state's argument that the statutory preference was meant to ease its probate courts' burden in adjudicating contests between family members:

> A classification "must be reasonable, not arbitrary, and must rest upon some ground of difference having a fair and substantial relation to the object of the legislation, so that all persons similarly circumstanced shall be treated alike." . . . Clearly the objective of reducing the workload on probate courts by eliminating one class of contests is not without some legitimacy. The crucial question, however, is whether [the preference statute] advances that objective in a manner consistent with the command of the Equal Protection Clause. We hold that it does not. To give a mandatory preference to members of either sex over members of the other, merely to accomplish the elimination of hearings on the merits, is to make the very kind of arbitrary legislative choice forbidden by the Equal Protection Clause of the Fourteenth Amendment; and whatever may be said as to the positive

values of avoiding intrafamily controversy, the choice in this context may not lawfully be mandated solely on the basis of sex.

The district court in *Frontiero* had interpreted *Reed* to hold merely that "a statutory presumption which had no relation to the statutory purpose" violated the Equal Protection Clause. The Frontieros, however, argued that *Reed* must have held that gender was a "suspect class" requiring that claims of gender-based discrimination be given closer, stricter scrutiny. Four Justices agreed with the Frontieros; they were willing to hold that "classifications based upon sex, like classifications based upon race, alienage, and national origin, are inherently suspect and must therefore be subjected to close judicial scrutiny," and did the best they could to demonstrate that *Reed* had so held. Four Justices, including Chief Justice [Warren E.] Burger who had authored the *Reed* decision, disagreed:

It is unnecessary for the Court in this case to characterize sex as a suspect classification, with all of the far-reaching implications of such a holding. *Reed v. Reed*, which abundantly supports our decision today, did not add sex to the narrowly limited group of classifications which are inherently suspect. .... [W]e can and should decide this case on the authority of *Reed* and reserve for the future any expansion of its rationale.

The Significance of *Frontiero*

Although the plurality opinion in *Frontiero* comes the closest so far to Supreme Court endorsement of the view that legislative classifications based on gender must overcome strict scrutiny to satisfy the demands of the equal-protection principle, the Court has been edging ever closer to that endorsement. Three years after *Frontiero*, a majority of the Supreme Court agreed that "classifications by gender must serve important governmental objectives and must be substantially related to achievement of those objectives" to overcome an equal-protection challenge. By 1988, a unanimous Court had coalesced around this "intermediate scrutiny" standard of review for gender-based classifications. In 1996, Justice [Ruth Bader] Ginsburg pushed a clear majority of the Court still further in the direction of the standard she had advocated as a young law professor, in *amicus* brief and oral argument on behalf of the ACLU, to the *Frontiero* Court (emphasis added):

> To summarize the Court's current directions for cases of official classification based on gender: Focusing on the differential treatment of denial of opportunity for which relief is sought, *the reviewing court must determine whether the proffered justification is "exceedingly persuasive."* The burden of justification is demanding and it rests entirely on the State. The State must show "at least that the challenged classification serves 'important governmental objectives and that the discriminatory means employed' are 'substantially related to the achievement of those objectives.'" The justification must be genuine, not hypothesized or invented *post hoc* in response to litigation. And it must not rely on overbroad generalizations about the different talents, capacities, or preferences of males and females.

Family law has long recognized the important roles that women play in our society as mothers, daughters, sisters, spouses, and friends. Full participation outside the home has been a goal that women have fought to achieve throughout recent history. Whether by pushing for voting rights, fighting for equal pay for equal work, or demanding equal treatment from the U.S. government with regard to the status of their dependents, women have made huge strides towards achieving this goal. The achievement of social equality for women has been a long journey. The Equal Rights Amendment, contrary to Justice [Lewis F.] Powell's half-prediction, was not ratified after *Frontiero*. So far as the Constitution's equal-protection principle is concerned, however, *Frontiero v. Richardson* represents one of the first and most important steps in that journey's path.

> "Women today serve in the military forces of many nations, and they are no longer limited to supporting roles."

The *Frontiero* Decision Helped Women Achieve Equality in the Military

Lory Manning

Lory Manning is a retired U.S. Navy captain and director of the Women in the Military Project at the Women's Research and Education Institute, a public policy research group in Washington.

In the following selection Manning contends that unlike in the past, women today have come to serve in the military in a variety of roles. Recounting the history of women in the U.S. military, Manning points out the significance of the Women's Armed Services Integration Act—as well as the subsequent chipping away of this act—to women's increased presence in the U.S. military. Among the significant court decisions, legislative acts, and service policies that paved the way for a higher rate of participation by women was the 1973 Court decision in Frontiero, *allowing servicewomen to collect benefits for their husbands in the same way that servicemen are allowed to get benefits for their wives.*

Quick, which employer in the United States can—indeed must—discriminate against its employees based solely on their gender, without regard for their actual skills and talents?

Lory Manning, "Military Women: Who They Are, What They Do, and Why It Matters," *The Women's Review of Books*, vol. 21, no. 5, February 2004, pp. 7–8. Copyright © 2004 Old City Publishing, Inc. Reproduced by permission.

If you answered the US military, you are right. This legal discrimination works against both sexes. Only men are required to register for the draft, and only women are prohibited from serving in the infantry, armor (such as tanks), most field artillery, special forces, and aboard submarines. War is, and has always been, a gendered pursuit. If you were a warrior, you were male; often, if you were male, you were a warrior. That logic is now coming apart in the United States and scores of other countries. Women today serve in the military forces of many nations, and they are no longer limited to supporting roles. Any discourse on women and war must acknowledge and discuss women as warriors, which means knowing something about who military women are, what they do, and how their roles have evolved.

Women in the Military

On September 30, 2003, according to the Defense Manpower Data Center (DMDC), there were 213,059 women (15 percent of the force) serving on active duty in the four Department of Defense services; 4,126 women serving in the active Coast Guard (10.7 percent)—part of the Department of Homeland Security; and 151,441 women (17.2 percent of the force) serving in the guard and reserve. Women are also entering the military at growing rates. According to DMDC, in fiscal year 2002, 18 percent of new army enlistees were women, as were 17 percent of the navy's, 7 percent of the marine corps' and 23 percent of the air force's. On the officer side, these percentages were 19 percent, 18 percent, 9 percent, and 23 percent, respectively.

Women join the military for the same reasons men do—for the education benefits, the job training, the chance to travel, and because military service is a family tradition—but there are demographic differences between military men and women, especially with regard to race and ethnicity. Just over one-third of enlisted men are from ethnic minority groups, but over 50 percent of enlisted women are (33.2 percent African American, 1.8 percent Native American, 4.1 percent Asian American, 10.2 percent Hispanic origin and 2.5 percent bi- or multi-racial). Among officers, 18.7 percent of the men are from minority groups, whereas about 30 percent of women officers are (16.2 percent African American, .7 percent Native American, 5.2 percent Asian American, 4.8 percent Hispanic origin, and 3.7 percent bi- or multi-racial). Women serve in every enlisted rank and in every officer rank except the four-star level—the highest rank now attainable—and chances are good that a woman will reach that rank within the next ten years. Women serve aboard—indeed, command—navy and coast guard ships, fly every sort of military aircraft, and serve in deployed army and marine corps units around the world. Over 10 percent of those serving in the current operations in Iraq are women.

Many who read these statistics will be astounded at the inroads women have quietly made into the supposedly males-only turf of the modern military in just over a century. The change began with a need for skilled nurses in both the Civil and Spanish-American Wars. The US government recruited women to serve as nurses with the army and navy, but these women retained their civilian status. By the end of the Spanish-American War, army leaders wanted both more women nurses and military authority over them. This led to the inclusion of a provision for a nurse corps in the Army Reorganization Act of 1901. The navy established its own nurse corps in 1908. The next key change—the movement of women into military jobs other than nursing—came during World War I. The navy and marine corps brought women—including a few African-American women—onto active duty to serve as typists, telephone operators, and translators. These women were released from active duty as soon as the war ended, but their use during wartime set a precedent that was built upon during World War II. Over 400,000 women served in that war in a wide range of military occupations, including gunnery instructors and mechanics. Over 400 American servicewomen died during the war, and 88 were held for several years as prisoners of war—all but one in the Pacific theater. The dedication and professional competence of these women convinced many military men, including Generals Eisenhower and Marshall, that the United States ought to keep a cadre of women on active duty in fields other than nursing after the war.

The Women's Armed Services Integration Act

This was accomplished through the passage of the Women's Armed Services Integration Act of 1948. People reading this legislation today will find it at best quaint and at worst downright patriarchal. They may wonder why any woman would choose to serve under its provisions. Yet for its time, it was radical. It allowed women other than nurses to serve in the peacetime armed forces and, after heated congressional debate, allowed them to hold regular commissions and to enter into regular enlistment contracts. This meant women could plan a career in the military free of the concern that they could be summarily released back to civilian life anytime the services felt like it. And—rare for 1948—women received pay equal to that of men of the same rank and length of service.

On the down side, the legislation limited women to no more than two percent of the total force and stipulated that women officers could be no more than ten percent of that two percent. It capped women officers' rank at lieutenant colonel/commander, although one woman in each service could hold the temporary rank of colonel/captain while serving as head of its women's branch. It precluded husbands from receiving healthcare benefits, family housing, and access to military commissary and exchange facilities unless they were dependent on their wives for over 50 percent of their support, and it prohibited women from serving aboard navy ships—except hospital and transport ships—and aboard any aircraft that could have a combat mission. Women who became pregnant or who even lived in a household in which a child under 18 was present for more than 30 days per year were required to leave the service. Women were also forbidden by service policy from having command authority over men. This meant that while women could have men working for them, they could not award nonjudicial punishment to men or order them to court-martial. Without this authority, women were effectively barred from commanding any military unit or facility in which men served.

The Removal of Limitations

Interestingly, while this legislation specifically barred women from air and sea combat, it placed no bar on their serving in ground combat. The legislators of 1948 speculated that at some future time an attempt might be made to place women aboard ships and in aircraft—hence, the bar—but it never occurred to them that serious thought could be given to involving women in ground combat occupations. Hence, there was no legislative bar, just a policy one.

Over the next 50 years, the limitations placed on women's service by the 1948 law were toppled one by one through actions of the courts, Congress, and the services themselves. In 1967, Congress removed the caps on women's numbers and ranks, clearing the way for women admirals and generals and, incidentally, for the end of male conscription. Since then, women's rate of participation has gradually grown from less than two percent to today's 15 percent and climbing. In 1972, the Supreme Court decision in *Frontiero v. Richardson* awarded the husbands of military women the same benefits as the wives of military men. A US Court of Appeals decision in the 1976 case *Crawford v. Cushman* found that regulations mandating the discharge of pregnant women violated their Fifth

Amendment rights. That same year, Congress opened the service academies to women. During the 1970s, each of the services rewrote its policies so that women could award nonjudicial punishment and courtmartial to men, thereby opening the way for women to command military units. The remaining two provisions of the 1948 law—the ban against women serving in aircraft with combat missions and aboard combat ships—were repealed by Congress in 1991 and 1994, respectively. Also in 1994, many previously closed army and marine corps units and positions were opened to women. Service assignment policies—which now require congressional notification before changes can be made—still bar US servicewomen from serving in ground combat units, although women from Canada, South Africa, and Germany can serve in these kinds of units. US women are also barred from service in submarines, although women in Canada, Australia, Sweden, and Norway serve in them.

Two Trends

Two trends are of particular interest. First, women are increasingly participating in the US and other militaries around the world. In the US and some other countries, their numbers and influence could approach critical mass over the next decade. Second, women from a growing number of countries are entering into combat arms occupations. Both these trends matter greatly, yet they have gone largely unremarked by feminist and other scholars.

The impact of the growing population of military women on institutional military cultures is already apparent, although how this manifests itself varies from nation to nation and service to service. It can be seen in the growing unwillingness of military women—and a lot of military men, too—to tolerate sexual assault, sexual harassment, or plain, old-fashioned sexism. Military equipment is more apt to be designed for operation by members of both sexes. Military medical researchers are looking at the impact of high-endurance physical activity on both sexes, studying the effects of heat, cold, dehydration, zero-gravity, high altitude, and exposure to hazardous substances. Military leaders are looking into better ways for male and female soldiers to integrate military service with family life.

The other trend—the opening of combat arms to women—is even more important, because national-level military leaders are drawn only from the combat arms branches in most countries, and these military leaders play a critical role in national and international decision-making on strategy, operations, and fiscal appropriations. It's conceivable that the US will have a woman member of the Joint Chiefs of Staff within the next decade or so. Women could also reach this level of influence in other countries where they serve in air, sea, or land combat, such as in most NATO countries, Australia, New Zealand, South Africa, India, South Korea, Singapore, Brazil, Israel, and Japan. Women have served as heads of state, heads of government, defense ministers, and in every sort of cabinet post and legislative office. They are judges, professional athletes, and bishops. They run NGOs [nongovernmental organizations], universities, and multinational corporations, but throughout modern history right up to today, not one woman has been a national-level military commander. Soon that will change. Our thinking about women and war must expand to encompass this change.

> "The majority ranked sexual orientation
> as warranting the magnifying glass of
> intermediate scrutiny, like gender is un-
> der the U.S. Constitution."

The Reasoning in *Frontiero* Protecting Women Supports Protection of Homosexuals

Thomas B. Scheffey

Thomas B. Scheffey is staff writer for the Connecticut Law Tribune.

*In the following selection Scheffey discusses both the signifi-
cant legislative decisions and judicial decisions leading up to the
Connecticut Supreme Court's decision in* Kerrigan v. Commissioner of Public Health *(2008). This court decision, by applying
heightened scrutiny, determined that prohibiting same-sex marriage violated the equal protection clause of the Connecticut
Constitution. Scheffey explains how the Connecticut court justified its use of heightened scrutiny to laws treating people differently according to sexual orientation by relying on the U.S. Supreme Court's reasoning in* Frontiero v. Richardson *(1973),
which applied heightened scrutiny to laws treating people differently according to sex.*

The Connecticut Supreme Court's ruling that same-sex
marriage is required under the state Constitution is the
product of years of advancing thought from lawmakers, jurists
and the general public.

The Road to Same-Sex Marriage in Connecticut

Rep. Michael P. Lawlor, co-chair of the legislative Judiciary Committee, is a strong proponent of marriage equality. "The part I'm happiest about is that the legislature and the courts were going down the same path at approximately the same pace for 10 years," he said.

The significant change began with the 1999 [Connecticut] Supreme Court case of *In Re the Adoption of Baby Z*, brought by a lesbian couple in Ledyard, Ann and Malinda. The baby was Ann's and Malinda was her life partner. The state Supreme Court ruled that no statute allowed Malinda to adopt Ann's child, tossing the issue to the legislature.

In the next session, a bill was crafted that would allow same-sex parent adoption, but it was freighted with a "defense of marriage amendment" [DOMA] asserting that only opposite sex unions would be recognized by the state.

Lawlor and others shelved that bill, and in the ensuing months a Hartford-based advocacy group known as Love Makes A Family was formed. Lawmakers were invited into the homes of constituents who were same-sex couples, many of whom had children. Minds, and votes, changed.

The next version of the bill lacked the DOMA language, and established Connecticut as a state that, as a matter of public policy, regarded same-sex couples as legally equal to heterosexual couples.

In his dissent from the 4-3 decision in *Kerrigan v. Commissioner of Health*, Justice Peter T. Zarella argued that the basis of marriage was procreation, not just love and long-term commitment. For that reason, he said, the state could have a strong regulatory interest focused on couples capable of giving birth to a baby. Using that reasoning, he stated that it should not be unconstitutional to have married heterosexual couples as one group, and homosexual couples as a different legal category.

"Zarella's argument that the legislature could give a preferred status to marriage because it's all about procreation is true," said Lawlor, "but that's not what we did."

The Name Distinction

In 2005, lawmakers launched a debate that would ultimately end in a bill allowing gay and lesbian couples to be joined in civil unions.

"We said everywhere in the statute books where you see the word marriage, put a comma, and add 'civil union,'" Lawlor said. In other words, civil union and marriage had different names, but in other respects they were to be treated exactly equally, he said.

But to some, the name distinction remained important. In 2005, opponents made a strong case that the term "marriage" was a treasured term of historic social importance, and should be denied to same-sex couples. Republican Sen. Lawrence Cafero, D-Norwalk, added an amendment that civil unions were never to be called marriage.

That opened the door for attorney Bennett Klein, who represented the eight same-sex couples who filed the *Kerrigan vs. Commissioner of Public Health* lawsuit that sought marriage rights. His philosophical adversaries in the legislature had eloquently made his point—that the term "marriage" itself had deep value.

In his arguments before the state Supreme Court on May 14, 2007, he suggested why "just a name" does matter. What if the first female judge in Connecticut were told she would have all the powers of a male judge, but because of her gender, she would be called a magistrate. Would that pass court scrutiny?, Bennett asked.

Justice David M. Borden, a former acting chief justice, dissented from the *Kerrigan* majority on grounds the plaintiffs had not produced evidence in the trial court record that civil union status had any less prestige than marriage. But the court majority ultimately held it unconstitutional to have separate designations for heterosexual and homosexual couples, even if the only distinction was the name.

Changing Minds

In the meantime, public opinion polls indicated that Connecticut residents, particularly the young, were becoming more accepting of same-sex couples. In early 2007, a University of Connecticut and Hartford Courant poll indicated that Connecticut residents favored same sex marriage 49 percent to 46 percent.

Meanwhile, a wide range of professional groups were rallying to the cause. The *Kerrigan* plaintiffs eventually attracted friend of the court briefs from the Connecticut Clergy for Marriage Equality, family lawyers, historians, legal scholars and professors.

In January 2007, Lawlor and Sen. Andrew J. McDonald, the other Judiciary Committee co-chair, introduced "An Act Concerning Marriage Equality," which defined marriage as "the legal union of two persons." After vigorous debate, the committee passed the marriage equality bill by a surprisingly comfortable 25 to 17 margin.

But there were not yet enough votes to bring it to a vote in the full General Assembly. "Some people said they needed a little more time to consider it," Lawlor said in an interview. "But it was clear to me then that it was only a matter of time."

The time came when the Kerrigan case, initially filed in 2004, reached the state Supreme Court in May 2007.

The Justification for Heightened Scrutiny

At the oral arguments, Assistant Attorney General Jane Rosenberg conceded that sexual orientation met two parts of a test for heightened court scrutiny, like laws based on race or religion. But she disagreed that gays and lesbians had a history of political powerlessness. "We now have civil union laws, and we now have prominent politicians who are openly gay," she said. Lawlor and McDonald are two of the most prominent, and powerful, who fit that category.

Justice Flemming L. Norcott Jr., answering Rosenberg, said: "It depends how you define political power. If it were true political power, they would have passed a bill across the street" in the legislature for same-sex marriage.

Justice Borden took Rosenberg's point about political power to heart, and centered his dissent on the fact that gays have made great strides in politics. For that reason alone, he argued, they should not enjoy the special protection of heightened court scrutiny the majority ruled they deserve.

But Justice Richard N. Palmer, writing for the majority, countered that some blacks were politically powerful in 1954, when the U.S. Supreme Court in *Brown v. Board of Education* struck down "separate but equal" schools. Likewise, many women had political power in 1973, when *Frontiero v. Richardson* made gender a protected classification.

The Connecticut court majority did not rank sexual orientation as highly as race, religion, color, national origin, or physical disability. Laws based on those classifications go under the microscope of strict court scrutiny for constitutionality. Instead, Palmer and the majority ranked sexual orientation as warranting the magnifying glass of intermediate scrutiny, like gender is under the U.S. Constitution.

The majority decision also chided Borden, saying that if he had been on the U.S. Supreme Court, his insistence on political powerlessness could have set back the cause of blacks and women.

National Model

Just as Connecticut's same-sex marriage decision was the culmination of years of legislative and judicial action, the ruling itself could set off its own chain of events.

Klein, a lawyer in the Boston office of Gay and Lesbian Defenders and Advocates, said this year's [2008's] California Supreme Court decision legalizing same-sex marriage [Proposition 8, passed later in 2008, overrode this decision] spent only five pages on its equal protection analysis, while the Connecticut majority opinion dug deep, for some 85 pages.

The Connecticut opinion is "the best roadmap for other courts to follow in deciding why sexual orientation distinctions in the law need to be subjected to heightened scrutiny," Klein said.

As a result, Lawlor said, the decision could attract attention in New Jersey, Vermont and New Hampshire, states which have civil unions but not marriage equality.

McDonald, in an interview, said there were many unanswered questions the legislature would need to clarify in the next session. But, he added, same-sex marriage should be available as early as next month.

He noted how the tide of public opinion has changed over the years toward acceptance of same-sex marriage. "This week," he said, "the latest UConn poll showed there were 54 percent in favor, 42 [percent] opposed. He also noted that Republican Gov. M. Jodi Rell, who had threatened to veto a same-sex marriage statute, said she wouldn't fight the Supreme Court decision."

CHAPTER 2

Striking Down Statutes Requiring Alimony Only of Men

Case Overview

Orr v. Orr (1979)

In *Orr v. Orr* the U.S. Supreme Court determined that the alimony statutes of Alabama constituted sex discrimination in violation of the equal protection clause of the Fourteenth Amendment. Six of the justices joined in the majority opinion, while three justices dissented.

When Mr. and Mrs. Orr divorced, Mr. Orr agreed to pay Mrs. Orr alimony. After the Alabama court ordered Mr. Orr to make the payments, Mr. Orr filed a petition alleging that the alimony statutes violated the equal protection clause of the Fourteenth Amendment by requiring alimony only from divorced men and not from divorced women. Both the trial court and court of appeals sustained the constitutionality of the statutes, but the Supreme Court reversed their decisions.

In its decision the Court found the state's three justifications for the different treatment of men and women within the statutes lacking. First the Court claimed that the state may not justify the alimony statutes by its preference for a family structure that involves a dependent wife—this goal was determined to be illegitimate. Second, although the Court did agree that the state could do its best to make sure that a needy spouse was not harmed by divorce, the Court claimed that the state could not rightfully assume that all women would need alimony due to their usual role in a marriage. The Court noted that the state already held hearings to determine financial circumstances of the two parties, so the state could also determine actual need rather than making a blanket assumption based on sex. Finally the Court agreed with the state that reducing the income disparities between men and women was an important goal but again held that individualized hearings could see to this goal without a blanket policy toward all divorced men and women. Thus the Court concluded that there was no legitimate goal served by treating men and women different with respect to alimony, finding such statutes to constitute unconstitutional sex discrimination. The three dissenting justices in this case argued that there was no equal protection issue in this case because Mr. Orr would be liable for alimony whether the law was gender-neutral or not.

Orr was significant because it limited the extent to which states could use family law to promote or discourage a certain kind of structure between men and women. Alimony laws currently differ from state to state, and alimony decisions are made on a case-by-case basis. Since *Orr*, however, those laws and decisions cannot use the sex of divorced individuals to determine their need or their duty to pay.

*"A gender-based classification which . . .
generates additional benefits only for
those it has no reason to prefer cannot
survive equal protection scrutiny."*

The Court's Decision:
Legislation Distributing
Benefits and Burdens by
Gender Is Unconstitutional

William J. Brennan Jr.

*William J. Brennan Jr. was appointed to the Supreme Court in
1956 by President Dwight D. Eisenhower and served until he re-
signed for health reasons in 1990.*

*The following is the majority opinion in the 1979 case of
Orr v. Orr, the Supreme Court ruling that reversed a lower
court decision upholding an Alabama alimony law requiring alimony from husbands to needy wives upon divorce but never
from wives to husbands. Writing for the Court, Justice Brennan
argues that Alabama's alimony statute is unconstitutional under
the equal protection clause of the Fourteenth Amendment because it only applies to men and not to women. Justice Brennan
notes that although the statute is unconstitutional, it is up to
Alabama to determine—under a gender-neutral framework—
whether or not Mr. Orr would need to pay alimony.*

The question presented is the constitutionality of Alabama
alimony statutes which provide that husbands, but not
wives, may be required to pay alimony upon divorce.

William J. Brennan Jr., majority opinion, *Orr v. Orr*, U.S. Supreme Court, 1979.

On February 26, 1974, a final decree of divorce was entered, dissolving the marriage of William and Lillian Orr. That decree directed appellant, Mr. Orr, to pay appellee, Mrs. Orr, $1,240 per month in alimony. On July 28, 1976, Mrs. Orr initiated a contempt proceeding in the Circuit Court of Lee County, Ala., alleging that Mr. Orr was in arrears in his alimony payments. On August 19, 1976, at the hearing on Mrs. Orr's petition, Mr. Orr submitted in his defense a motion requesting that Alabama's alimony statutes be declared unconstitutional because they authorize courts to place an obligation of alimony upon husbands, but never upon wives. The Circuit Court denied Mr. Orr's motion and entered judgment against him for $5,524, covering back alimony and attorney fees. Relying solely upon his federal constitutional claim, Mr. Orr appealed the judgment. On March 16, 1977, the Court of Civil Appeals of Alabama sustained the constitutionality of the Alabama statutes. On May 24, the Supreme Court of Alabama granted Mr. Orr's petition for a writ of certiorari [review of the lower court], but on November 10, without court opinion, quashed the writ as improvidently granted. We noted probable jurisdiction. We now hold the challenged Alabama statutes unconstitutional, and reverse.

We first address three preliminary questions not raised by the parties or the Alabama courts below, but which nevertheless may be jurisdictional, and therefore are considered of our own motion.

The Legal Standing of Mr. Orr

The first concerns the standing of Mr. Orr to assert in his defense the unconstitutionality of the Alabama statutes. It appears that Mr. Orr made no claim that he was entitled to an award of alimony from Mrs. Orr, but only that he should not be required to pay alimony if similarly situated wives could not be ordered to pay. It is therefore possible that his success here will not ultimately bring him relief from the judgment outstanding against him, as the State could respond to a reversal by neutrally extending alimony rights to needy husbands, as well as wives. In that event, Mr. Orr would remain obligated to his wife. It is thus argued that the only "proper plaintiff" would be a husband who requested alimony for himself, and not one who merely objected to paying alimony.

This argument quite clearly proves too much. In every equal protection attack upon a statute challenged as underinclusive, the State may satisfy the Constitution's commands either by extending benefits to the previously disfavored class or by denying benefits to both parties (e.g., by repealing the statute as a whole). In this case, if held unconstitutional, the Alabama divorce statutes could be validated by, inter alia [among other things], amendments which either (1) permit awards to husbands as well as wives or (2) deny alimony to both parties. It is true that, under the first disposition, Mr. Orr might gain nothing from his success in this Court, although the hypothetical "requesting" plaintiff would. However, if, instead, the State takes the second course and denies alimony to both spouses, it is Mr. Orr, and not the hypothetical plaintiff, who would benefit. Because we have no way of knowing how the State will, in fact, respond, unless we are to hold that underinclusive statutes can never be challenged because any plaintiff's success can theoretically be thwarted, Mr. Orr must be held to have standing here. We have on several occasions considered this inherent problem of challenges to underinclusive statutes, and have not denied a plaintiff standing on this ground.

There is no question but that Mr. Orr bears a burden he would not bear were he female. The issue is highlighted, although not altered, by transposing it to the sphere of race. There is no doubt that a state law imposing alimony obligations on blacks but not whites could be challenged by a black who was required to pay. The burden alone is sufficient to establish standing. Our resolution of a statute's constitutionality often does "not finally resolve the controversy as between

th[e] appellant and th[e] appellee" [*Stanton v. Stanton* (1975)].
We do not deny standing simply because the "appellant, although prevailing here on the federal constitutional issue, may
or may not ultimately win [his] lawsuit." The holdings of the
Alabama courts stand as a total bar to appellant's relief; his
constitutional attack holds the only promise of escape from
the burden that derives from the challenged statutes. He has
therefore alleged such a personal stake in the outcome of the
controversy as to assure that concrete adverseness which sharp-
ens the presentation of issues upon which th[is] court so
largely depends for illumination of difficult constitutional
questions [*Linda R. S. v. Richard D.* (1973), quoting *Baker v.
Carr* (1962)]. Indeed, on indistinguishable facts, this Court
has stated that a party's standing will be sustained. In *Linda R.
S. v. Richard D.*, we stated that the parent of a legitimate child
who must by statute pay child support has standing to challenge the statute on the ground that the parent of an illegitimate child is not equally burdened.

The Timeliness of Mr. Orr's Challenge

A second preliminary question concerns the timeliness of
appellant's challenge to the constitutionality of the statutes.
No constitutional challenge was made at the time of the original divorce decree; Mr. Orr did not interpose the Constitution
until his ex-wife sought a contempt judgment against him for
his failure to abide by the terms of the decree. This unexcused
tardiness might well have constituted a procedural default under state law, and if Alabama had refused to hear Mr. Orr's
constitutional objection on that ground, we might have been
without jurisdiction to consider it here.

But, in this case, neither Mrs. Orr nor the Alabama courts
at any time objected to the timeliness of the presentation of
the constitutional issue. Instead, the Alabama Circuit and Civil
Appeals Courts both considered the issue to be properly pre-

sented, and decided it on the merits. In such circumstances, the objection that Mr. Orr's complaint

"comes too late" . . . is clearly untenable. . . . [S]ince the state court deemed the federal constitutional question to be before it, we could not treat the decision below as resting upon an adequate and independent state ground even if we were to conclude that the state court might properly have relied upon such a ground to avoid deciding the federal question [*Beecher v. Alabama* (1967)].

This is merely an application of the

elementary rule that it is irrelevant to inquire . . . when a Federal question was raised in a court below when it appears that such question was actually considered and decided [*Manhattan Life Ins. Co. v. Cohen* (1914)].

A Constitutional Question

The third preliminary question arises from indications in the record that Mr. Orr's alimony obligation was part of a stipulation entered into by the parties, which was then incorporated into the divorce decree by the Lee County Circuit Court. Thus, it may be that, despite the unconstitutionality of the alimony statutes, Mr. Orr may have a continuing obligation to his former wife based upon that agreement—in essence, a matter of state contract law. If the Alabama courts had so held, and had anchored their judgments in this case on that basis, an independent and adequate state ground might exist and we would be without power to hear the constitutional argument. And if there were ambiguity as to whether the State's decision was based on federal or state grounds, it would be open to this Court not to determine the federal question, but to remand to the state courts for clarification as to the ground of the decision.

But there is no ambiguity here. At no time did Mrs. Orr raise the stipulation as a possible alternative ground in support of her judgment. Indeed, her brief in the Alabama Court of Civil Appeals expressly stated that

> [t]he appellee agrees that the issue before this Court is whether the Alabama alimony laws are unconstitutional because of the gender based classification made in the statutes.

The Alabama Circuit and Civil Appeals Courts reached and decided the federal question without considering any state law issues, the latter specifying that

> [t]he sole issue before this court is whether Alabama's alimony statutes are unconstitutional. We find they are not unconstitutional, and affirm.

While no reason was given by the State Supreme Court's majority for quashing the writ of certiorari, the concurring and dissenting opinions mention only the federal constitutional issue and do not mention the stipulation. And Mrs. Orr did not even raise the point in this Court. On this record, then, our course is clear and dictated by a long line of decisions.

> Where the state court does not decide against a petitioner or appellant upon an independent state ground, but deeming the federal question to be before it, actually entertains and decides that question adversely to the federal right asserted, this Court has jurisdiction to review the judgment if, as here, it is a final judgment. We cannot refuse jurisdiction because the state court might have based its decision, consistently with the record, upon an independent and adequate nonfederal ground [*Indiana ex rel. Anderson v. Brand* (1938)].

Our analysis of these three preliminary questions, therefore, indicates that we do have jurisdiction over the constitutional challenge asserted by Mr. Orr. As an Art. III "case or controversy" has been properly presented to this Court, we now turn to the merits.

The Dependent Wife Objective

In authorizing the imposition of alimony obligations on husbands, but not on wives, the Alabama statutory scheme

> provides that different treatment be accorded . . . on the basis of . . . sex; it thus establishes a classification subject to scrutiny under the Equal Protection Clause [*Reed v. Reed* (1971)].

The fact that the classification expressly discriminates against men, rather than women, does not protect it from scrutiny. "To withstand scrutiny" under the Equal Protection Clause,

> "classifications by gender must serve important governmental objectives, and must be substantially related to achievement of those objectives" [*Califano v. Webster* (1977)].

We shall, therefore, examine the three governmental objectives that might arguably be served by Alabama's statutory scheme.

Appellant views the Alabama alimony statutes as effectively announcing the State's preference for an allocation of family responsibilities under which the wife plays a dependent role, and as seeking for their objective the reinforcement of that model among the State's citizens. We agree, as he urges, that prior cases settle that this purpose cannot sustain the statutes. *Stanton v. Stanton* held that the "old notio[n]" that "generally it is the man's primary responsibility to provide a home and its essentials" can no longer justify a statute that discriminates on the basis of gender. "No longer is the female destined solely for the home and the rearing of the family, and only the male for the marketplace and the world of ideas." If the statute is to survive constitutional attack, therefore, it must be validated on some other basis.

The Needy Spouse Objective

The opinion of the Alabama Court of Civil Appeals suggests other purposes that the statute may serve. Its opinion states that the Alabama statutes were "designed" for "the wife of a broken marriage who needs financial assistance." This may be read as asserting either of two legislative objectives. One is a legislative purpose to provide help for needy spouses, using sex as a proxy for need. The other is a goal of compensating women for past discrimination during marriage, which assert-edly has left them unprepared to fend for themselves in the working world following divorce. We concede, of course, that assisting needy spouses is a legitimate and important govern-mental objective. We have also recognized

> [r]eduction of the disparity in economic condition between men and women caused by the long history of discrimina-tion against women ... as ... an important governmental objective [*Califano v. Webster*].

It only remains, therefore, to determine whether the classifica-tion at issue here is "substantially related to achievement of those objectives."

Ordinarily, we would begin the analysis of the "needy spouse" objective by considering whether sex is a sufficiently "accurate proxy" [*Craig v. Boren* (1976)] for dependency to es-tablish that the gender classification rests "'upon some ground of difference having a fair and substantial relation to the ob-ject of the legislation'" [*Reed v. Reed*]. Similarly, we would ini-tially approach the "compensation" rationale by asking whether women had, in fact, been significantly discriminated against in the sphere to which the statute applied a sex-based classifica-tion, leaving the sexes "not similarly situated with respect to opportunities" in that sphere [*Schlesinger v. Ballard* (1975)].

But in this case, even if sex were a reliable proxy for need, and even if the institution of marriage did discriminate against women, these factors still would "not adequately justify the sa-lient features of" Alabama's statutory scheme [*Craig v. Boren*]. Under the statute, individualized hearings at which the parties' relative financial circumstances are considered already occur. There is no reason, therefore, to use sex as a proxy for need. Needy males could be helped along with needy females with little if any additional burden on the State. In such circumstances, not even an administrative convenience rationale exists to justify operating by generalization or proxy. Similarly, since individualized hearings can determine which women were, in fact, discriminated against *vis-a-vis* [in relation to] their husbands, as well as which family units defied the stereotype and left the husband dependent on the wife, Alabama's alleged compensatory purpose may be effectuated without placing burdens solely on husbands. Progress toward fulfilling such a purpose would not be hampered, and it would cost the State nothing more, if it were to treat men and women equally by making alimony burdens independent of sex.

> Thus, the gender-based distinction is gratuitous; without it, the statutory scheme would only provide benefits to those men who are, in fact, similarly situated to the women the statute aids [*Weinberger v. Wiesenfeld* (1975)]

and the effort to help those women would not in any way be compromised.

The Perverse Results of the Statute

Moreover, use of a gender classification actually produces perverse results in this case. As compared to a gender-neutral law placing alimony obligations on the spouse able to pay, the present Alabama statutes give an advantage only to the financially secure wife whose husband is in need. Although such a wife might have to pay alimony under a gender-neutral statute, the present statutes exempt her from that obligation. Thus, "[t]he [wives] who benefit from the disparate treatment are those who were . . . nondependent on their husbands" [*Califano v. Goldfarb* (1977)]. They are precisely those who are not "needy spouses" and who are "least likely to have been victims of . . . discrimination" by the institution of marriage. A gender-based classification which, as compared to a gender-neutral one, generates additional benefits only for those it has no reason to prefer cannot survive equal protection scrutiny.

Legislative classifications which distribute benefits and burdens on the basis of gender carry the inherent risk of reinforcing stereotypes about the "proper place" of women and their need for special protection. Thus, even statutes purportedly designed to compensate for and ameliorate the effects of past discrimination must be carefully tailored. Where, as here, the State's compensatory and ameliorative purposes are as well served by a gender-neutral classification as one that gender classifies, and therefore carries with it the baggage of sexual stereotypes, the State cannot be permitted to classify on the basis of sex. And this is doubly so where the choice made by the State appears to redound—if only indirectly—to the benefit of those without need for special solicitude.

An Unconstitutional Statute

Having found Alabama's alimony statutes unconstitutional, we reverse the judgment below and remand the cause for further proceedings not inconsistent with this opinion. That disposition, of course, leaves the state courts free to decide any questions of substantive state law not yet passed upon in this litigation. Therefore, it is open to the Alabama courts on remand to consider whether Mr. Orr's stipulated agreement to pay alimony, or other grounds of gender-neutral state law, bind him to continue his alimony payments.

| "It is not our duty to establish Orr's
| standing to have his claim decided on
| the merits."

Dissenting Opinion: No Sex Discrimination Exists for an Individual Who Is Not Harmed

William H. Rehnquist

William H. Rehnquist was a Supreme Court justice for thirty-three years (from 1972 to 2005), the last nineteen of which he served as chief justice. Rehnquist was considered a conservative member of the Court.

In the following dissenting opinion from the 1979 case of Orr v. Orr, *Justice Rehnquist argues that the Supreme Court erred in finding unconstitutional the Alabama alimony law requiring alimony from husbands to needy wives upon divorce but never from wives to husbands. Rehnquist contends that in order for Mr. Orr to have standing—that is, a legitimate legal case—he would need to show that the law treating men and women differently resulted in injury to him that would be remedied by implementing a gender-neutral law. Rehnquist claims that Mr. Orr would be liable for alimony either way and thus concludes that there is no legitimate equal protection issue in this particular case.*

In Alabama, only wives may be awarded alimony upon divorce. In Part I of its opinion, the Court holds that Alabama's alimony statutes may be challenged in this Court

William H. Rehnquist, dissenting opinion, *Orr v. Orr*, U.S. Supreme Court, 1979.

by a divorced male who has never sought alimony, who is demonstrably not entitled to alimony even if he had, and who contractually bound himself to pay alimony to his former wife and did so without objection for over two years. I think the Court's eagerness to invalidate Alabama's statutes has led it to deal too casually with the "case and controversy" requirement of Art. III of the Constitution.

The Requirement for Case or Controversy

The architects of our constitutional form of government, to assure that courts exercising the "judicial power of the United States" would not trench upon the authority committed to the other branches of government, consciously limited the Judicial Branch's "right of expounding the Constitution" to "cases of a Judiciary Nature"—that is, to actual "cases" and "controversies" between genuinely adverse parties. Central to this Art. III limitation on federal judicial power is the concept of standing. The standing inquiry focuses on the party before the Court, asking whether he has

> "such a personal stake in the outcome of the controversy" as to warrant *his* invocation of federal court jurisdiction and to justify exercise of the court's remedial powers on his behalf [*Warth v. Seldin* (1975) (emphasis in original), quoting *Baker v. Carr* (1962)]. Implicit in the concept of standing are the requirements of injury in fact and causation. To demonstrate the "personal stake" in the litigation necessary to satisfy Art. III, the party must suffer "a distinct and palpable injury" [*Warth v. Seldin*] that bears a "'fairly traceable' causal connection" to the challenged government action [*Duke Power Co. v. Carolina Environmental Study Group, Inc.* (1978), quoting *Arlington Heights v. Metropolitan Housing Dev. Corp.* (1977)]. When a party's standing to raise an issue is questioned, therefore, "the relevant inquiry is whether . . . [he] has shown an injury to himself that is likely to be redressed by a favorable decision" [*Simon v. Eastern Kentucky Welfare Rights Org.* (1976)]. Stated differently, a party who

places a question before a federal court must "stand to profit in some personal interest" from its resolution, else the exercise of judicial power would be gratuitous.

The sole claim before this Court is that Alabama's alimony statutes, which provide that only husbands may be required to pay alimony upon divorce, violate the Equal Protection Clause of the Fourteenth Amendment. Statutes alleged to create an impermissible gender-based classification are generally attacked on one of two theories. First, the challenged classification may confer on members of one sex a benefit not conferred on similarly situated members of the other sex. Clearly, members of the excluded class—those who, but for their sex, would be entitled to the statute's benefits—have a sufficient "personal stake" in the outcome of an equal protection challenge to the statute to invoke the power of the federal judiciary. Thus, a widower has standing to question the constitutionality of a state statute granting a property tax exemption only to widows. Likewise, this Court has reached the merits of a retired male wage earner's equal protection challenge to a federal statute granting higher monthly old-age benefits to similarly situated female wage earners. . . .

Second, the challenged statute may saddle members of one sex with a burden not borne by similarly situated members of the other sex. Standing to attack such a statute lies in those who labor under its burden. For example, in *Califano v. Goldfarb* (1977), this Court sustained a widower's equal protection challenge to a provision of the Social Security Act that burdened widowers, but not widows, with the task of proving dependency upon the deceased spouse in order to qualify for survivor's benefits. A similar statute was invalidated in *Frontiero v. Richardson* (1973), at the instance of a female member of the uniformed services who, unlike her male counterparts, was required to prove her spouse's dependency in order to obtain increased quarters allowances and health benefits.

The statutes at issue here differ from those discussed above in that the benefit flowing to divorced wives derives from a burden imposed on divorced husbands. Thus, Alabama's alimony statutes in effect create two gender classifications: that between needy wives, who can be awarded alimony under the statutes, and needy husbands, who cannot; and that between financially secure husbands, who can be required to pay alimony under the statutes, and financially secure wives, who cannot. Appellant Orr's standing to raise his equal protection claim must therefore be analyzed in terms of both of these classifications.

The Situation of Mr. Orr

This Court has long held that, in order to satisfy the "injury in fact" requirement of Art. III standing, a party claiming that a statute unconstitutionally withholds a particular benefit must be in line to receive the benefit if the suit is successful. In *Supervisors v. Stanley* (1882), shareholders of a national bank attacked the validity of a state property tax statute that did not, contrary to federal law, permit deduction of personal debts from the assessed value of their bank stock. With respect to the constitutional claim of shareholders who had failed to allege the existence of personal debts that could be deducted under a valid statute, the Court reasoned:

> What is there to render the [state statute] void as to a shareholder in a national bank, who owes no debts which he can deduct from the assessed value of his shares? The denial of this right does not affect him. He pays the same amount of tax that he would if the law gave him the right of deduction. He would be in no better condition if the law expressly authorized him to make the deduction. What legal interest has he in a question which only affects others? Why should he invoke the protection of the act of Congress in a case where he has no rights to protect? Is a court to sit and de-

cide abstract questions of law in which the parties before it show no interest, and which, if decided either way, affect no right of theirs?

... If no such right exists, the delicate duty of declaring by this court that an act of State legislation is void, is an assumption of authority uncalled for by the merits of the case, and unnecessary to the assertion of the rights of any party to the suit.

It is undisputed that the parties now before us are "a needy wife who qualifies for alimony and a husband who has the property and earnings from which alimony can be paid." Under the statute pertinent to the Orrs' divorce, alimony may be awarded against the husband only "[i]f the wife has no separate estate or if it be insufficient for her maintenance." At the time of their divorce, Mr. Orr made no claim that he was not in a position to contribute to his needy wife's support, much less that she should be required to pay alimony to him. On the contrary, the amount of alimony awarded by the Alabama trial court was agreed to by the parties, and appellant has never sought a reduction in his alimony obligation on the ground of changed financial circumstances. On these facts, it is clear that appellant is not in a position to benefit from a sex-neutral alimony statute. His standing to raise the constitutional question in this case, therefore, cannot be founded on a claim that he would, but for his sex, be entitled to an award of alimony from his wife under the Alabama statutes.

Mr. Orr's Alimony Obligation

The Court holds that Mr. Orr's standing to raise his equal protection claim lies in the burden he bears under the Alabama statutes. He is required to pay alimony to his needy former spouse, while similarly situated women are not. That the State may render Mr. Orr's victory in this Court a hollow one by neutrally extending alimony rights to needy husbands does not, according to the Court, destroy his standing, for the

State may elect instead to do away with alimony altogether. The possibility that Alabama will turn its back on the thousands of women currently dependent on alimony checks for their support is, as a practical matter, nonexistent. But my conclusion that appellant lacks standing in this Court does not rest on the strong likelihood that Alabama will respond to today's decision by passing a sex-neutral statute. Appellant has simply not demonstrated that either alternative open to the State—even the entire abrogation of alimony—will free him of his burden.

The alimony obligation at issue in this case was fixed by an agreement between the parties, and appellant makes no claim that the contract is unenforceable under state law. Indeed, the Court itself concedes that "despite the unconstitutionality of the alimony statutes, Mr. Orr may have a continuing obligation to his former wife based upon [their] agreement." The Court casually dismisses the matter, however, as one "which we cannot, and would not, predict."

I cannot accede to the Court's offhand dismissal of so serious an obstacle to the exercise of our jurisdiction. It is not our duty to establish Orr's standing to have his claim decided on the merits. On the contrary, the burden is on him

> to meet the minimum requirement of Art. III: to establish that, in fact, the asserted injury was the consequence of the [unconstitutional statute], or that prospective relief will remove the harm [*Warth v. Seldin* (1975)]. That appellant has not carried this burden is clearly demonstrated by the Court's acknowledgment that his alimony obligation may well be enforced under state contract law.

A Lack of Support for the Court's Conclusion

The Court's analysis of Mr. Orr's standing is not aided by its attempt to transform the instant case into one involving race discrimination. Of course, a state law imposing alimony obligations on blacks but not whites could be challenged by a black required, by operation of the statute, to pay alimony. Invalidation of the discriminatory alimony statute would relieve him of his burden. If, however, his alimony obligation was enforceable under state contract law independent of the challenged alimony statute, he could hardly argue that his injury was caused by the challenged statute. Invalidation of the statute would bring him no relief. Accordingly, the exercise of federal judicial power on his behalf "would be gratuitous, and thus inconsistent with the Art. III limitation" [*Simon v. Eastern Kentucky Welfare Rights Org.* (1976)].

Nor is the Court's conclusion supported by *Linda R. S. v. Richard D.* [1973]. At issue in *Linda R. S.* was a state statute subjecting to criminal prosecution any "parent" failing to support his "children." State courts had consistently construed the statute to apply solely to the parents of legitimate children and to impose no duty of support on the parents of illegitimate children. The mother of an illegitimate child, claiming that the "discriminatory application" of the statute violated the Equal Protection Clause, sought an injunction directing the local district attorney to prosecute the father of her child for violating the statute. This Court held that she lacked standing to raise her claim. While she "no doubt suffered an injury stemming from the failure of her child's father to contribute support payments," she had made

> no showing that her failure to secure support payments result[ed] from the nonenforcement, as to her child's father, of [the child support statute]. . . .

> Thus, if appellant were granted the requested relief, it would result only in the jailing of the child's father. The prospect that prosecution will, at least in the future, result in payment of support can, at best, be termed only speculative. Certainly the "direct" relationship between the alleged injury

and the claim sought to be adjudicated which previous decisions of this Court suggest is a prerequisite of standing, is absent in this case.

Like appellant in *Linda R. S.*, Mr. Orr has failed to show a "substantial likelihood" that the requested relief will result in termination of his alimony obligation. Thus, far from supporting the Court's finding of standing in appellant Orr, *Linda R. S.* leads inescapably to the opposite conclusion.

The Power of Federal Courts

Nor is appellant's lack of standing somehow cured by the fact that the state courts reached and decided the merits of his constitutional claim. Article III is a jurisdictional limitation on federal courts, and a state court cannot transform an abstract or hypothetical question into a "case or controversy" merely by ruling on its merits. In *Doremus v. Board of Education* (1952), this Court held that a taxpayer lacked the requisite financial interest in the outcome of a First Amendment challenge to a state statute requiring Bible reading in public schools. In dismissing the taxpayer's appeal from an adverse ruling in the State's highest court, this Court held:

> We do not undertake to say that a state court may not render an opinion on a federal constitutional question even under such circumstances that it can be regarded only as advisory. But, because our own jurisdiction is cast in terms of "case or controversy," we cannot accept as the basis for review, nor as the basis for conclusive disposition of an issue of federal law without review, any procedure which does not constitute such.

Appellant's case, having come to us on appeal, rather than on writ of certiorari [a request to review a lower court's findings], is much like Marbury's case, in that Congress conferred upon each litigant the right to have his claim heard in this Court. But here, as in *Marbury v. Madison* (1803), and *Dore-*

mus, we are, in my opinion, prevented by Art. III of the Constitution from exercising the jurisdiction which Congress has sought to confer upon us.

Article III courts are not commissioned to roam at large, gratuitously righting perceived wrongs and vindicating claimed rights. They must await the suit of one whose advocacy is inspired by a "personal stake" in victory. The Framers' wise insistence that those who invoke the power of a federal court personally stand to profit from its exercise ensures that constitutional issues are not decided in advance of necessity, and that the complaining party stand in the shoes of those whose rights he champions. Obedience to the rules of standing—the "threshold determinants of the propriety of judicial intervention"—is of crucial importance to constitutional adjudication in this Court, for when the parties leave these halls, what is done cannot be undone except by constitutional amendment.

> "In the nearly 30 years since the U.S. Supreme Court ruled against gender discrimination in alimony, few male beneficiaries have stepped forward to talk about it."

Men Receiving Alimony Still Suffer Stigmatization Years After *Orr*

Anita Raghavan

Anita Raghavan is European bureau chief in London for Forbes.
In the following article Raghavan reports that even a few decades after the Supreme Court's decision in Orr v. Orr *(1979), which required alimony laws to be gender neutral, there is still a stigma attached to divorced men who received alimony from their former wives. Raghavan claims that men offer many of the same classic reasons for alimony that women do, although many women who pay alimony are unhappy with the arrangement. The stigma attached to alimony for men along with the distaste many women feel in paying it, Raghavan claims, results in divorce settlements that aim to avoid alimony altogether.*

As a Hollywood actor, John David Castellanos is protective of his image. He stays in phenomenal shape and looks much younger than his 50 years.

But he admits to a fact that might be considered unflattering: He receives alimony from his former wife. To be exact, $9,000 a month.

Anita Raghavan, "Men Receiving Alimony Want a Little Respect," *Wall Street Journal*, April 1, 2008, p. A1. Reprinted with permission of *The Wall Street Journal*.

"The law provides" for it, says Mr. Castellanos, who for years starred in the soap opera "The Young and the Restless."

The Stigma of Alimony for Men

In the nearly 30 years since the U.S. Supreme Court ruled against gender discrimination in alimony, few male beneficiaries have stepped forward to talk about it. Those who did typically went by pseudonyms or the golden rule of 12-step recovery: first names only.

Little wonder, considering the attention that has come to some former husbands of alimony-paying celebrities. "Why the courts don't tell a husband, who has been living off his wife, to go out and get a job is beyond my comprehension," Joan Lunden, the television personality, said in 1992 when a court ordered her to pay her ex-husband $18,000 a month.

But today's men are shaking off the stigma of being supported by their ex-wives. Several agreed to talk on the record for this article, in part because they say the popular image of the male alimony recipient is unfair: He's not always a slacker.

Mr. Castellanos says he has acted in or produced five movies since the breakup of his marriage, including a couple of projects that he says are nearing completion. If any of these projects strike gold, he says he would gladly forgo alimony. Even Ms. Lunden has had a change of heart. Through a former publicist, she now says of her 1992 comment: "That was a statement made in haste many years ago. I regret having said it."

Divorce experts say that fewer and fewer men are rejecting outright any talk of seeking alimony. The percentage of alimony recipients who are male rose to 3.6% during the five years ending in 2006, up from 2.4%, in the previous five-year period, according to the U.S. Census Bureau.

That percentage is likely to rise as more and more marriages feature a primary earner who is female. In 2005 (the latest year for which data are available), wives outearned their husbands in 33% of all families, up from 28.2% a decade earlier.

Alimony—a distinctly different category from child support—is the money that higher-earning spouses hand to their lower-earning counterparts following the end of their marriage. Often it is court-ordered, years in duration and based on big discrepancies in spousal incomes.

Classic Reasons for Alimony

Today, men in growing numbers are receiving alimony for the classic reasons that women traditionally did. A common argument is that they sacrificed their careers for the sake of their wives'.

"If it was not for the joint decision to support Marjorie's career advancement to the detriment of mine, I would be making considerably more money than I am currently," Christopher Bowen argued in a 2005 filing in Los Angeles Superior Court.

At the time of that request, Mr. Bowen was a Wachovia Securities executive receiving about $550,000 in annual pay, according to the court documents. But his wife, Marjorie Bowen, was expected in 2005 to earn $1.5 million as an executive at investment-banking boutique Houlihan Lokey Howard & Zukin, according to the court documents.

Mr. Bowen argued in the filing that when the couple moved back to Los Angeles because of her career opportunities, he took a cut in pay. "Based on my salary alone, I cannot maintain the marital standard of living," Mr. Bowen wrote in a petition filed in the Los Angeles court in August 2005.

Male alimony seekers are also touting sacrifices made on behalf of children. In the marriage of Joe and Diane Garnick, she logged 12-hour days as a global equity derivatives strategist for Merrill Lynch, earning several times what Mr. Garnick did as a top-performing toilet salesman. So in 2001, he quit that job to focus on raising their two girls, keeping the house clean and doing the shopping.

Following his 2002 divorce, he received alimony of $50,000 a year for four years from Ms. Garnick, now an investment strategist at Invesco Ltd.

As a stay-at-home dad, Mr. Garnick notes that he missed out on career opportunities that would have boosted his earning potential, particularly those involving travel. "I couldn't [travel] while I had a kid," Mr. Garnick says.

Mr. Garnick used the alimony to earn a mathematics degree from a community college. But he has returned to his old job selling toilets, where he earns only half what he did before quitting. "Society thinks that just because you are a man you can pick up a career after you have dropped it for 10 years and jump right back," he says. "That's just not the case."

Men and Women, and Alimony

Still, relatives of his former wife continue referring to Mr. Garnick as a "deadbeat," he says. And Ms. Garnick herself says, "In some instances, alimony has become akin to a social-welfare program provided by working women to their ex-husbands."

Some feminists say cases such as Mr. Garnick's show progress of a sort. "We can't assert rights for women and say that men aren't entitled to the same rights," says the famous feminist lawyer, Gloria Allred.

But the women who have to pay it are sounding a different chord. "I feel financially raped," says Rhonda Friedman, the former wife of Mr. Castellanos. So distasteful are the monthly payments she makes to him that after filling out the check she used to spit on it. Especially galling, she says, is that she was required to pay a substantial portion of the legal fees he racked up while securing a lucrative divorce agreement.

Avoiding Alimony

To be sure, some men don't want alimony, viewing it as an embarrassment. Others are just as high-powered as their wives. Yahoo President Susan Decker and her soon-to-be ex-husband have taken alimony off the table, according to court records. Meanwhile, Sara Lee Chief Executive Brenda Barnes is paying no alimony to her ex-husband, a former PepsiCo Inc. executive who now manages his own money. Until their youngest child recently turned 18, Ms. Barnes, who earned a total of $8.7 million in fiscal 2007, was receiving child-support payments from her former husband, according to court records.

Other men have learned that alimony is a powerful negotiating tactic, especially when their estranged wives clearly want to sever all ties. "For some people, it is truly offensive to write out a check each month to a spouse for support," says Sue Moss, a divorce lawyer at Chemtob Moss Forman & Talbert LLP in New York. "In those instances, if you can offer a financial package that is essentially the same as if maintenance was being paid, it is the preferable alternative."

Indeed, the increasingly common practice of trading alimony for a fatter slice of marital assets helps explain why the overall number of people reporting alimony income fell 17% during the decade ended in 2006, to a total of fewer than 400,000, the Census Bureau says.

In the case of Wachovia's Mr. Bowen, he ultimately waived his rights to spousal support. But the resulting settlement—which neither party will publicly discuss—suggests that Mr. Bowen received a generous division of assets. In addition to half of his wife's substantial private-equity investments, Mr. Bowen received a home in Manhattan Beach, Calif., a parcel in Utah and some properties in Brooklyn, N.Y.

Disputes About Alimony

Soap star Mr. Castellanos bluntly says he deserves alimony for the same reason that his former wife, Ms. Friedman, says he doesn't: He earned more than she did during six of the nine years they were married. Only after losing his regular role on "The Young and the Restless," and only after his wife received several promotions, did she start earning more than he. For years, his big paychecks financed their lavish lifestyle, and now he is due some payback, he says.

To Ms. Friedman, that financial history fails to support the argument that she should send thousands a month to her ex-husband, with whom she had no children. "I don't understand why someone becomes your financial responsibility just because you married them," says Ms. Friedman, who earns about $500,000 a year as the supervising producer of the soap opera "The Bold and the Beautiful."

Mr. Castellanos also argues that as an artist, he provided his wife with invaluable advice and insight that helped Ms. Friedman rise from production coordinator to producer.

Ms. Friedman hotly denies that he had anything to do with her success.

Even men without marital sacrifices to cite as cause for alimony are coming around to the idea that good fortune is no cause for shame. Women, after all, have been crowing for decades about the financial scalpings they collect monthly from their ex-husbands. So why shouldn't Phillip Upton take pride in his classic "muscle cars"?

A shop foreman at the time of his divorce last year, Mr. Upton says he couldn't have afforded the $20,000-a-year cost of maintaining his 1960s-vintage collection of cars with out-sized motors.

But in his divorce settlement, he won alimony payments totaling at least $40,000 a year from his ex-wife, a marketing executive. "Had I not gotten that, I would have lived a different lifestyle," says Mr. Upton. His former wife, Noreen Upton, declined to comment.

| *"Right or not, as women's earnings grow, so will their financial responsibility during divorce."*

Women Are Increasingly Paying Alimony as Equality Requires

Betsy Schiffman

Betsy Schiffman is a writer who has written articles for publications such as Forbes, Pink, *and the* San Francisco Chronicle.

In the following article Schiffman recounts how the equality in alimony law established by Orr v. Orr (1979) is still not palatable to many women and men, a few decades after the decision. Because women are making more money than ever and often outearning their husbands, Schiffman argues, alimony payments from women to their former husbands have become increasingly common in recent years. She notes that despite this, many women do not respond well to the request for alimony from them, and many men are still reluctant to seek alimony. Nonetheless, Schiffman concludes, equality demands that women pay alimony in the same cases where men would be required to pay alimony.

The picture of equality looks awfully strange to Kim Shamsky. The 47-year-old business owner pays her ex, a 65-year-old retired Major League Baseball player, thousands per month in temporary spousal support.

Betsy Schiffman, "Women Increasingly Paying Alimony," *Forbes*, March 13, 2007. Reproduced by permission.

The Rise in Alimony for Men

He's not seeking alimony to help pay for the kids' birthday parties, since they don't have children. Nor was he instrumental in building her business. They married seven years after she started a handful of staffing firms and amassed a small fortune on her own. The daughter of a New York City taxi driver, Shamsky started her first staffing agency at age 27 with the help of a 21% loan. Not only was she able to make her first business profitable, but she's also worked furiously to ensure the success of all five businesses she's started since. Small wonder she is outraged at having to pay thousands of dollars a month to her ex.

"He used to scream and throw tantrums and demand more money," Shamsky says of her ex-husband. "It was like he thought, 'Hey, you have money, why shouldn't I?'" She adds flatly: "I will never marry again. And I'm getting T-shirts made with the word 'prenup' written across the chest."

No doubt Shamsky would find more than a few buyers for the shirts. The idea that men can receive spousal support from their wives may feel like a freakish concept, but as women have become higher earners, it's increasingly common.

Women's Responses to Alimony

And as men set their sights on women's earnings, women have become more protective of those dollars. In fact, according to the American Academy of Matrimonial Lawyers, 44% of attorneys included in a recent survey said they've seen an increase in women asking for prenuptial agreements over the last five years, where in previous decades, prenuptial agreements were almost always sought by men.

A lot of women are indignant now that the shoe is increasingly on the other foot, says Carol Ann Wilson, a certified financial divorce practitioner in Boulder, Colo. "There's this sense of, 'What's yours is ours, but what's mine is mine,'" Wilson says. "My first response to that is, 'All these years we have been looking for equality; well, this is what it looks like.' I think women get angrier about having to pay than men do."

The ordeal has been played up in gossip magazines and tabloids, which have closely followed countless examples of celebrity breakups in which men have sought, or have threatened to seek, spousal support. Teen idol and crooner Nick Lachey reportedly requested the right to seek spousal support from ex-wife pop singer Jessica Simpson last year [2006]. (Lachey is seven years older than Simpson and reportedly worth significantly less.) In another splashy case, Hardy Boy Parker Stevenson sought $18,000 per month from actress Kirstie Alley when they divorced, just to cover the rent on his Bel Air home.

But Wilson emphasizes that it's not just actresses or the wealthiest women who are seeking prenuptial agreements or paying spousal support. "I've seen thousands of clients," she says, "and almost every time I've seen a stay-at-home dad seek alimony, the wife—she's usually a software executive—goes ballistic."

Some women find it's not a battle worth fighting, according to Cheryl Lynn Hepfer, the Rockville, Md.-based president of the American Academy of Matrimonial Lawyers. Hepfer says she's seen women who have happily chosen to pay off their husbands in an effort to maintain their sanity and keep the peace.

"I once represented a wealthy woman who had the wherewithal to pay $6,000 a month to her husband—and this was probably 10 years ago—so she paid him," Hepfer says, adding that the client also gave her ex the boat and the house on the water. "She wasn't bitter about it at all. She was a business woman, and for her, this was a business decision." Hepfer says she did it to preserve the relationship with her former husband and their two children. "She knew it would be beneficial for the kids."

Men's Responses to Alimony

Just as some women object to men's request for spousal support, some men are particularly uncomfortable seeking it. Either they find it emasculating to ask, or they find the idea of receiving an allowance from their ex-wives humiliating, according to divorce attorneys.

"The fact is that you still don't see too many cases where men seek alimony," says William Beslow, a divorce attorney in New York City. "One reason is that although women may earn more than men, they often wind up with custody of the children, and when a woman takes up primary responsibility for the children, men don't request maintenance."

Some men avoid the embarrassment by seeking a bigger bite of the marital assets instead of asking for alimony. Not only do lump-sum payments save them the humiliation of accepting monthly support, but they also reduce the ex-husband's taxes, since spousal support payments are taxed, while assets are not.

The Price of Equality

On the flip side, in those situations when men receive assets, women lose their tax benefit, because spousal support is tax-deductible, Hepfer notes. The upshot: Even if it's easier to settle with one swift payment, consult an accountant first to learn the tax consequences. It may be better for you financially to pay alimony.

Kim Shamsky admits she's angry about paying her ex-husband spousal support mostly because he's a man. After all, men are supposed to be breadwinners, not bread takers.

"A real man just wouldn't do this sort of thing," she says. "Maybe it's my Italian upbringing, but I don't think it's right."

Right or not, as women's earnings grow, so will their financial responsibility during divorce. That's equality for you.

CHAPTER 3

Upholding
Affirmative Action for
Working Women

Case Overview

Johnson v. Transportation Agency (1987)

In *Johnson v. Transportation Agency* the U.S. Supreme Court determined that an affirmative action plan that used sex as a factor in making hiring and promoting decisions was not in violation of Title VII of the Civil Rights Act of 1964. Although the Court had in the past ruled against laws and policies where considerations of sex were used discriminatorily in hiring decisions, the Court determined in this case that sex can be considered as a factor in employment when doing so has the goal of remedying past discrimination and underrepresentation of women in the workforce.

In 1979 the Transportation Agency of Santa Clara County, California, announced a vacancy for the job of road dispatcher, a Skilled Craft Worker position. Of the 238 jobs in the agency's Skilled Craft Worker category at the time, not one was held by a woman. Twelve people applied for the job, and Paul Johnson, a man, and Diana Joyce, a woman, were the leading candidates. The interviewers rated both as well qualified, although Johnson had a higher interview score than Joyce. The agency decided to hire Joyce for the position, its decision partly influenced by its goal of increasing the number of women hired, trained, and promoted by the agency.

Paul Johnson filed a complaint with the U.S. Equal Employment Opportunity Commission (EEOC) alleging a sex discrimination violation of Title VII of the Civil Rights Act of 1964, which prohibits employment discrimination based on race, color, religion, sex, or national origin in regard to hiring, termination, promotion, compensation, job training, or any other condition of employment. Johnson brought suit to the district court, which ruled that the agency's affirmative action plan was inconsistent with Title VII. The court of appeals then reversed the district court's ruling, finding the affirmative action plan that took account of Joyce's sex in her hiring to be consistent with Title VII. On appeal to the Supreme Court, the court of appeals decision was upheld.

The Court found that the affirmative action plan at issue in *Johnson* did not violate Title VII but in fact furthered Title VII's purpose of eliminating the effects of discrimination in the workplace. The Court found that the agency's affirmative action plan was legitimate because it established a long-term goal of having more women in positions at the agency without establishing strict quotas—the Court made clear that sex could not legitimately be the only consideration in employment decisions. Furthermore the Court concluded that the affirmative action plan in question did not discriminate against men because sex was merely used as one deciding factor among otherwise qualified applicants, in an attempt to eliminate the remnants of years of discrimination against women.

Johnson was significant, as it was the first case to test the legality of sex-based affirmative action plans under Title VII. The Court's decision in this case endorsed affirmative action as a remedy for past sex discrimination, as long as such affirmative action is temporary. Justice Antonin Scalia's dissent in this case echoes a view widely held today, that taking account of sex is not the right path to a society free of sex discrimination. With respect to affirmative action based on race, the Court in 2003 upheld the use of race in making law school admissions decisions, in *Grutter v. Bollinger*; but in *Parents Involved in Community Schools v. Seattle School District No. 1* (2007), the Court prohibited the assignment of students to public school by race in order to achieve racial integration. Given the Court's insistence that affirmative action programs be temporary, presumably the day will come when such programs will be seen as constituting sex discrimination that is incompatible with law.

"Such a plan is fully consistent with Title VII, for it embodies the contribution that voluntary employer action can make in eliminating the vestiges of discrimination in the workplace."

The Court's Decision: Taking Account of Sex in Order to Eliminate Underrepresentation in Employment Is Constitutional

William J. Brennan Jr.

William J. Brennan Jr. was a justice of the U.S. Supreme Court from 1956 to 1990. He was an outspoken liberal and is considered to be one of the more influential justices to have sat on the Supreme Court.

The following is the majority opinion in the 1987 case of Johnson v. Transportation Agency, *wherein the Supreme Court decided that hiring policies by employers that take account of sex are constitutionally permissible if they are an effort to eliminate historic underrepresentation of women in particular jobs caused by past discrimination. Writing for the majority, Brennan affirmed a decision of the lower court of appeals that had determined the affirmative action plan of the agency in question was not in violation of Title VII of the Civil Rights Act of 1964, which prohibits discrimination in employment on the basis of sex.*

William J. Brennan Jr., majority opinion, *Johnson v. Transportation Agency*, U.S. Supreme Court, 1987.

In December 1978, the Santa Clara County Transit District Board of Supervisors adopted an Affirmative Action Plan (Plan) for the County Transportation Agency. The Plan implemented a County Affirmative Action Plan, which had been adopted, declared the County, because

> mere prohibition of discriminatory practices is not enough to remedy the effects of past practices and to permit attainment of an equitable representation of minorities, women and handicapped persons.

Relevant to this case, the Agency Plan provides that, in making promotions to positions within a traditionally segregated job classification in which women have been significantly underrepresented, the Agency is authorized to consider as one factor the sex of a qualified applicant.

Reasons for the Plan

In reviewing the composition of its workforce, the Agency noted in its Plan that women were represented in numbers far less than their proportion of the County labor force in both the Agency as a whole and in five of seven job categories. Specifically, while women constituted 36.4% of the area labor market, they composed only 22.4% of Agency employees. Furthermore, women working at the Agency were concentrated largely in EEOC [U.S. Equal Employment Opportunity Commission] job categories traditionally held by women: women made up 76% of Office and Clerical Workers, but only 7.1% of Agency Officials and Administrators, 8.6% of Professionals, 9.7% of Technicians, and 22% of Service and Maintenance Workers. As for the job classification relevant to this case, none of the 238 Skilled Craft Worker positions was held by a woman. The Plan noted that this underrepresentation of women in part reflected the fact that women had not traditionally been employed in these positions, and that they had not been strongly motivated to seek training or employment in them "because of the limited opportunities that have existed in the past for them to work in such classifications." The Plan also observed that, while the proportion of ethnic minorities in the Agency as a whole exceeded the proportion of such minorities in the County workforce, a smaller percentage of minority employees held management, professional, and technical positions.

The Agency stated that its Plan was intended to achieve

> a statistically measurable yearly improvement in hiring, training and promotion of minorities and women throughout the Agency in all major job classifications where they are underrepresented.

As a benchmark by which to evaluate progress, the Agency stated that its long-term goal was to attain a workforce whose composition reflected the proportion of minorities and women in the area labor force. Thus, for the Skilled Craft category in which the road dispatcher position at issue here was classified, the Agency's aspiration was that, eventually, about 36% of the jobs would be occupied by women.

The Goals of the Plan

The Plan acknowledged that a number of factors might make it unrealistic to rely on the Agency's long-term goals in evaluating the Agency's progress in expanding job opportunities for minorities and women. Among the factors identified were low turnover rates in some classifications, the fact that some jobs involved heavy labor, the small number of positions within some job categories, the limited number of entry positions leading to the Technical and Skilled Craft classifications, and the limited number of minorities and women qualified for positions requiring specialized training and experience. As a result, the Plan counseled that short-range goals be established and annually adjusted to serve as the most realistic guide for actual employment decisions. Among the tasks identified as important in establishing such short-term goals was the acquisition of data reflecting the ratio of minorities, women and handicapped persons who are working in the local area in major job classifications relating to those utilized by the County Administration,

so as to determine the availability of members of such groups who "possess the desired qualifications or potential for placement." These data on qualified group members, along with predictions of position vacancies, were to serve as the basis for

realistic yearly employment goals for women, minorities and handicapped persons in each EEOC job category and major job classification.

The Agency's Plan thus set aside no specific number of positions for minorities or women, but authorized the consideration of ethnicity or sex as a factor when evaluating qualified candidates for jobs in which members of such groups were poorly represented. One such job was the road dispatcher position that is the subject of the dispute in this case.

The Skilled Craft Worker Job

On December 12, 1979, the Agency announced a vacancy for the promotional position of road dispatcher in the Agency's Roads Division. Dispatchers assign road crews, equipment, and materials, and maintain records pertaining to road maintenance jobs. The position requires, at minimum, four years of dispatch or road maintenance work experience for Santa Clara County. The EEOC job classification scheme designates a road dispatcher as a Skilled Craft Worker.

Twelve County employees applied for the promotion, including Joyce and Johnson. Joyce had worked for the County since 1970, serving as an account clerk until 1975. She had applied for a road dispatcher position in 1974, but was deemed ineligible because she had not served as a road maintenance worker. In 1975, Joyce transferred from a senior account clerk position to a road maintenance worker position, becoming the first woman to fill such a job. During her four years in that position, she occasionally worked out of class as a road dispatcher.

Petitioner Johnson began with the County in 1967 as a road yard clerk, after private employment that included working as a supervisor and dispatcher. He had also unsuccessfully applied for the road dispatcher opening in 1974. In 1977, his clerical position was downgraded, and he sought and received a transfer to the position of road maintenance worker. He also occasionally worked out of class as a dispatcher while performing that job.

Choice of a Candidate

Nine of the applicants, including Joyce and Johnson, were deemed qualified for the job, and were interviewed by a two-person board. Seven of the applicants scored above 70 on this interview, which meant that they were certified as eligible for selection by the appointing authority. The scores awarded ranged from 70 to 80. Johnson was tied for second with a score of 75, while Joyce ranked next with a score of 73. A second interview was conducted by three Agency supervisors, who ultimately recommended that Johnson be promoted. Prior to the second interview, Joyce had contacted the County's Affirmative Action Office because she feared that her application might not receive disinterested review. The Office in turn contacted the Agency's Affirmative Action Coordinator, whom the Agency's Plan makes responsible for, *inter alia* [among other things], keeping the Director informed of opportunities for the Agency to accomplish its objectives under the Plan. At the time, the Agency employed no women in any Skilled Craft position, and had never employed a woman as a road dispatcher. The Coordinator recommended to the Director of the Agency, James Graebner, that Joyce be promoted.

Graebner, authorized to choose any of the seven persons deemed eligible, thus had the benefit of suggestions by the

second interview panel and by the Agency Coordinator in arriving at his decision. After deliberation, Graebner concluded
that the promotion should be given to Joyce. As he testified:

> I tried to look at the whole picture, the combination of her
> qualifications and Mr. Johnson's qualifications, their test
> scores, their expertise, their background, affirmative action
> matters, things like that. . . . I believe it was a combination
> of all those.

The certification form naming Joyce as the person promoted to the dispatcher position stated that both she and
Johnson were rated as well qualified for the job. The evaluation of Joyce read:

> Well qualified by virtue of 18 years of past clerical experi-
> ence, including 3 1/2 years at West Yard plus almost 5 years
> as a [road maintenance worker].

The evaluation of Johnson was as follows:

> Well qualified applicant; two years of [road maintenance
> worker] experience plus 11 years of Road Yard Clerk. Has
> had previous outside Dispatch experience, but was 13 years
> ago.

Graebner testified that he did not regard as significant the fact
that Johnson scored 75 and Joyce 73 when interviewed by the
two-person board.

The Case in Lower Courts

Petitioner Johnson filed a complaint with the EEOC, alleging
that he had been denied promotion on the basis of sex in violation of Title VII. He received a right-to-sue letter from the
EEOC on March 10, 1981, and on March 20, 1981, filed suit
in the United States District Court for the Northern District
of California. The District Court found that Johnson was
more qualified for the dispatcher position than Joyce, and that
the sex of Joyce was the "*determining factor* in her selection."

The court acknowledged that, since the Agency justified its decision on the basis of its Affirmative Action Plan, the criteria announced in *Steelworkers v. Weber* (1979) should be applied in evaluating the validity of the Plan. It then found the Agency's Plan invalid on the ground that the evidence did not satisfy *Weber*'s criterion that the Plan be temporary. The Court of Appeals for the Ninth Circuit reversed, holding that the absence of an express termination date in the Plan was not dispositive, since the Plan repeatedly expressed its objective as the attainment, rather than the maintenance, of a workforce mirroring the labor force in the County. The Court of Appeals added that the fact that the Plan established no fixed percentage of positions for minorities or women made it less essential that the Plan contain a relatively explicit deadline. The Court held further that the Agency's consideration of Joyce's sex in filling the road dispatcher position was lawful. The Agency Plan had been adopted, the court said, to address a conspicuous imbalance in the Agency's workforce, and neither unnecessarily trammeled the rights of other employees nor created an absolute bar to their advancement. . . .

In reviewing the employment decision at issue in this case, we must first examine whether that decision was made pursuant to a plan prompted by concerns similar to those of the employer in *Weber*. Next, we must determine whether the effect of the Plan on males and nonminorities is comparable to the effect of the plan in that case.

The Issue of Underrepresentation

The first issue is therefore whether consideration of the sex of applicants for Skilled Craft jobs was justified by the existence of a "manifest imbalance" that reflected underrepresentation of women in "traditionally segregated job categories." In determining whether an imbalance exists that would justify taking sex or race into account, a comparison of the percentage of minorities or women in the employer's workforce with the percentage in the area labor market or general population is appropriate in analyzing jobs that require no special expertise, or training programs designed to provide expertise. Where a job requires special training, however, the comparison should be with those in the labor force who possess the relevant qualifications. The requirement that the "manifest imbalance" relate to a "traditionally segregated job category" provides assurance both that sex or race will be taken into account in a manner consistent with Title VII's purpose of eliminating the effects of employment discrimination, and that the interests of those employees not benefiting from the plan will not be unduly infringed. . . .

It is clear that the decision to hire Joyce was made pursuant to an Agency plan that directed that sex or race be taken into account for the purpose of remedying underrepresentation. The Agency Plan acknowledged the "limited opportunities that have existed in the past," for women to find employment in certain job classifications "where women have not been traditionally employed in significant numbers." As a result, observed the Plan, women were concentrated in traditionally female jobs in the Agency, and represented a lower percentage in other job classifications than would be expected if such traditional segregation had not occurred. Specifically, 9 of the 10 Para-Professionals and 110 of the 145 Office and Clerical Workers were women. By contrast, women were only 2 of the 28 Officials and Administrators, 5 of the 58 Professionals, 12 of the 124 Technicians, none of the Skilled Craft Workers, and 1—who was Joyce—of the 110 Road Maintenance Workers. The Plan sought to remedy these imbalances through "hiring, training and promotion of . . . women throughout the Agency in all major job classifications where they are underrepresented."

The Agency's Goals

As an initial matter, the Agency adopted as a benchmark for measuring progress in eliminating underrepresentation the long-term goal of a workforce that mirrored in its major job classifications the percentage of women in the area labor market. Even as it did so, however, the Agency acknowledged that such a figure could not by itself necessarily justify taking into account the sex of applicants for positions in all job categories. For positions requiring specialized training and experience, the Plan observed that the number of minorities and women "who possess the qualifications required for entry into such job classifications is limited." The Plan therefore directed that annual short-term goals be formulated that would provide a more realistic indication of the degree to which sex should be taken into account in filling particular positions. The Plan stressed that such goals "should not be construed as 'quotas' that must be met," but as reasonable aspirations in correcting the imbalance in the Agency's workforce. These goals were to take into account factors such as

> turnover, layoffs, lateral transfers, new job openings, retirements and availability of minorities, women and handicapped persons in the area workforce who possess the desired qualifications or potential for placement.

The Plan specifically directed that, in establishing such goals, the Agency work with the County Planning Department and other sources in attempting to compile data on the percentage of minorities and women in the local labor force that were actually working in the job classifications constituting the Agency workforce. From the outset, therefore, the Plan sought annually to develop even more refined measures of the underrepresentation in each job category that required attention.

As the Agency Plan recognized, women were most egregiously underrepresented in the Skilled Craft job category, since none of the 238 positions was occupied by a woman. In mid-1980, when Joyce was selected for the road dispatcher position, the Agency was still in the process of refining its short-term goals for Skilled Craft Workers in accordance with the directive of the Plan. This process did not reach fruition until

1982, when the Agency established a short-term goal for that year of 3 women for the 55 expected openings in that job category—a modest goal of about 6% for that category.

We reject petitioner's argument that, since only the long-term goal was in place for Skilled Craft positions at the time of Joyce's promotion, it was inappropriate for the Director to take into account affirmative action considerations in filling the road dispatcher position. The Agency's Plan emphasized that the long-term goals were not to be taken as guides for actual hiring decisions, but that supervisors were to consider a host of practical factors in seeking to meet affirmative action objectives, including the fact that, in some job categories, women were not qualified in numbers comparable to their representation in the labor force. . . .

The Rights of Male Employees

We next consider whether the Agency Plan unnecessarily trammeled the rights of male employees or created an absolute bar to their advancement. In contrast to the plan in *Weber*, which provided that 50% of the positions in the craft training program were exclusively for blacks, and to the consent decree upheld last Term in *Firefighters v. Cleveland* (1986), which required the promotion of specific numbers of minorities, the Plan sets aside no positions for women. The Plan expressly states that "[t]he 'goals' established for each Division should not be construed as 'quotas' that must be met." Rather, the Plan merely authorizes that consideration be given to affirmative action concerns when evaluating qualified applicants. As the Agency Director testified, the sex of Joyce was but one of numerous factors he took into account in arriving at his decision. The Plan thus resembles the "Harvard Plan" approvingly noted by JUSTICE [Lewis F.] POWELL in *Regents of University of California v. Bakke* (1978), which considers race along with other criteria in determining admission to the college. As JUSTICE POWELL observed:

In such an admissions program, race or ethnic background may be deemed a "plus" in a particular applicant's file, yet it does not insulate the individual from comparison with all other candidates for the available seats.

Similarly, the Agency Plan requires women to compete with all other qualified applicants. No persons are automatically excluded from consideration; *all* are able to have their qualifications weighed against those of other applicants.

In addition, petitioner had no absolute entitlement to the road dispatcher position. Seven of the applicants were classified as qualified and eligible, and the Agency Director was authorized to promote any of the seven. Thus, denial of the promotion unsettled no legitimate, firmly rooted expectation on the part of petitioner. Furthermore, while petitioner in this case was denied a promotion, he retained his employment with the Agency, at the same salary and with the same seniority, and remained eligible for other promotions. . . .

A Constitutional Affirmative Action Plan

The Agency has identified a conspicuous imbalance in job categories traditionally segregated by race and sex. It has made clear from the outset, however, that employment decisions may not be justified solely by reference to this imbalance, but must rest on a multitude of practical, realistic factors. It has therefore committed itself to annual adjustment of goals, so as to provide a reasonable guide for actual hiring and promotion decisions. The Agency earmarks no positions for anyone; sex is but one of several factors that may be taken into account in evaluating qualified applicants for a position. As both the Plan's language and its manner of operation attest, the Agency has no intention of establishing a workforce whose permanent composition is dictated by rigid numerical standards.

We therefore hold that the Agency appropriately took into account as one factor the sex of Diane Joyce in determining that she should be promoted to the road dispatcher position.

The decision to do so was made pursuant to an affirmative action plan that represents a moderate, flexible, case-by-case approach to effecting a gradual improvement in the representation of minorities and women in the Agency's workforce. Such a plan is fully consistent with Title VII, for it embodies the contribution that voluntary employer action can make in eliminating the vestiges of discrimination in the workplace.

"We effectively replace the goal of a discrimination-free society with the quite incompatible goal of proportionate representation by race and by sex in the workplace."

Dissenting Opinion: In Employment, Taking Sex into Account for Any Reason Is Sex Discrimination

Antonin Scalia

Antonin Scalia has been a member of the U.S. Supreme Court since 1986, when he was appointed by President Ronald Reagan. He is known for his conservatism, in general, and his commitment to the doctrine of originalism in interpreting the U.S. Constitution, in particular.

In the following excerpt from his dissent in the 1987 case of Johnson v. Transportation Agency, *Justice Scalia claims that there is never a justification for taking a person's sex into account in employment hiring decisions. The Court's reasoning in this case, Scalia claims, is inconsistent with the facts of the case. Rather than attempting to remedy past discrimination, argues Scalia, the affirmative action program in question in this case attempts to mirror the gender of employees in the community. Scalia concludes that such a policy contradicts Title VII of the Civil Rights Act of 1964, which demands that people not be discriminated against in hiring decisions because of their sex.*

Antonin Scalia, dissenting opinion, *Johnson v. Transportation Agency*, U.S. Supreme Court, 1987.

With a clarity which, had it not proven so unavailing, one might well recommend as a model of statutory drafts-manship, Title VII of the Civil Rights Act of 1964 declares:

It shall be an unlawful employment practice for an employer—

1. to fail or refuse to hire or to discharge any individual, or otherwise to discriminate against any individual with respect to his compensation, terms, conditions, or privileges of employment, because of such individual's race, color, religion, sex, or national origin; or

2. to limit, segregate, or classify his employees or applicants for employment in any way which would deprive or tend to deprive any individual of employment opportunities or otherwise adversely affect his status as an employee, because of such individual's race, color, religion, sex, or national origin.

The Court today completes the process of converting this from a guarantee that race or sex will *not* be the basis for employment determinations to a guarantee that it often *will*. Ever so subtly, without even alluding to the last obstacles preserved by earlier opinions that we now push out of our path, we effectively replace the goal of a discrimination-free society with the quite incompatible goal of proportionate representation by race and by sex in the workplace. . . .

The Affirmative Action Plan

On October 16, 1979, the County of Santa Clara adopted an Affirmative Action Program (County plan) which sought the

attainment of a County workforce whose composition . . . includes women, disabled persons and ethnic minorities in a ratio in all job categories that reflects their distribution in the Santa Clara County area workforce.

In order to comply with the County plan and various requirements imposed by federal and state agencies, the Transportation Agency adopted, effective December 18, 1978, the Equal Employment Opportunity Affirmative Action Plan (Agency plan or plan) at issue here. Its stated long-range goal was the same as the County plan's:

> to attain a workforce whose composition in all job levels and major job classifications approximates the distribution of women, minority and handicapped persons in the Santa Clara County workforce.

The plan called for the establishment of a procedure by which Division Directors would review the ethnic and sexual composition of their workforces whenever they sought to fill a vacancy, which procedure was expected to include

> a requirement that Division Directors indicate why they did *not* select minorities, women and handicapped persons if such persons were on the list of eligibles considered and if the Division had an underrepresentation of such persons in the job classification being filled.

The Plan and Past Sex Discrimination

Several salient features of the plan should be noted. Most importantly, the plan's purpose was assuredly not to remedy prior sex discrimination by the Agency. It could not have been, because there was no prior sex discrimination to remedy. The majority, in cataloging the Agency's alleged misdeeds, neglects to mention the District Court's finding that the Agency

> has not discriminated in the past, and does not discriminate in the present against women in regard to employment opportunities in general and promotions in particular.

This finding was not disturbed by the Ninth Circuit.

Not only was the plan not directed at the results of past sex discrimination by the Agency, but its objective was not to

achieve the state of affairs that this Court has dubiously as-
sumed would result from an absence of discrimination—an
overall workforce "more or less representative of the racial and
ethnic composition of the population in the community"
[*Teamsters v. United States* (1997)]. Rather, the oft-stated goal
was to mirror the racial and sexual composition of the entire
county labor force, not merely in the Agency workforce as a
whole, but in each and every individual job category at the
Agency. In a discrimination-free world, it would obviously be
a statistical oddity for every job category to match the racial
and sexual composition of even that portion of the county
workforce *qualified* for that job; it would be utterly miracu-
lous for each of them to match, as the plan expected, the
composition of the *entire* workforce. Quite obviously, the plan
did not seek to replicate what a lack of discrimination would
produce, but rather imposed racial and sexual tailoring that
would, in defiance of normal expectations and laws of prob-
ability, give each protected racial and sexual group a govern-
mentally determined "proper" proportion of each job category.

That the plan was not directed at remedying or eliminating the effects of past discrimination is most clearly illustrated
by its description of what it regarded as the "*Factors Hindering
Goal Attainment*"—i.e., the existing impediments to the ra-
cially and sexually representative workforce that it pursued.
The plan noted that it would be "difficult" to attain its objective of across-the-board statistical parity in at least some job
categories, because:

> a. Most of the positions require specialized training and ex-
> perience. Until recently, relatively few minorities, women
> and handicapped persons sought entry into these positions.
> Consequently, the number of persons from these groups in
> the area labor force who possess the qualifications required
> for entry into such job classifications is limited. . . .

c. Many of the Agency positions where women are under-represented involve heavy labor; *e.g.*, Road Maintenance Worker. Consequently, few women seek entry into these positions. . . .

f. Many women are not strongly motivated to seek employ-ment in job classifications where they have not been tradi-tionally employed because of the limited opportunities that have existed in the past for them to work in such classifica-tions.

That is, the qualifications and desires of women may fail to match the Agency's Platonic ideal of a workforce. The plan concluded from this, of course, not that the ideal should be reconsidered, but that its attainment could not be immediate. It would, in any event, be rigorously pursued, by giving

special consideration to Affirmative Action requirements in every individual hiring action pertaining to positions where minorities, women and handicapped persons continue to be underrepresented.

The Goal of Concrete Results

Finally, the one message that the plan unmistakably commu-nicated was that concrete results were expected, and supervi-sory personnel would be evaluated on the basis of the affir-mative action numbers they produced. The plan's implementation was expected to

result in a statistically measurable yearly improvement in the hiring, training and promotion of minorities, women and handicapped persons in the major job classifications utilized by the Agency where these groups are underrepresented.

Its Preface declared that

[t]he degree to which each Agency Division *attains the Plan's objectives* will provide a direct measure of that Division Director's personal commitment to the EEO Policy [empha-sis added],

and the plan itself repeated that

> [t]he degree to which each Division *attains the Agency Affirmative Action employment goals* will provide a measure of that Director's commitment and effectiveness in carrying out the Division's EEO Affirmative Action requirements [emphasis added].

As noted earlier, supervisors were reminded of the need to give attention to affirmative action in every employment decision, and to explain their reasons for *failing* to hire women and minorities whenever there was an opportunity to do so.

Sex Discrimination Against Johnson

The petitioner in the present case, Paul E. Johnson, had been an employee of the Agency since 1967, coming there from a private company where he had been a road dispatcher for 17 years. He had first applied for the position of Road Dispatcher at the Agency in 1974, coming in second. Several years later, after a reorganization resulted in a downgrading of his Road Yard Clerk II position, in which Johnson "could see no future," he requested and received a voluntary demotion from Road Yard Clerk II to Road Maintenance Worker, to increase his experience and thus improve his chances for future promotion. When the Road Dispatcher job next became vacant, in 1979, he was the leading candidate—and indeed was assigned to work out of class full-time in the vacancy, from September 1979 until June 1980. There is no question why he did not get the job.

The fact of discrimination against Johnson is much clearer, and its degree more shocking, than the majority and JUSTICE [Sandra Day] O'CONNOR's concurrence would suggest— largely because neither of them recites a single one of the District Court findings that govern this appeal, relying instead upon portions of the transcript which those findings implicitly rejected, and even upon a document (favorably comparing Joyce to Johnson) that was prepared *after* Joyce was selected.

Worth mentioning, for example, is the trier of fact's determination that, if the Affirmative Action Coordinator had not intervened, "the decision as to whom to promote . . . would have been made by [the Road Operations Division Director]," who had recommended that Johnson be appointed to the position. Likewise, the even more extraordinary findings that James Graebner, the Agency Director who made the appointment, "did not inspect the applications and related examination records of either [Paul Johnson] or Diane Joyce before making his decision," and indeed

> did little or nothing to inquire into the results of the interview process and conclusions which [were] described as of critical importance to the selection process.

In light of these determinations, it is impossible to believe (or to think that the District Court believed) Graebner's self-serving statements relied upon by the majority and JUSTICE O'CONNOR's concurrence, such as the assertion that he

> tried to look at the whole picture, the combination of [Joyce's] qualifications and Mr. Johnson's qualifications, their test scores, their expertise, their background, affirmative action matters, things like that,

It was evidently enough for Graebner to know that both candidates (in the words of Johnson's counsel, to which Graebner assented) "met the M.Q.'s, the minimum. Both were minimally qualified." When asked whether he had "any basis," for determining whether one of the candidates was more qualified than the other, Graebner candidly answered, "No. . . . As I've said, they both appeared, and my conversations with people tended to corroborate, that they were both capable of performing the work."

After a 2-day trial, the District Court concluded that Diane Joyce's gender was "*the determining factor*" in her selection for the position. Specifically, it found that,

[b]ased upon the examination results and the departmental interview, [Mr. Johnson] was more qualified for the position of Road Dispatcher than Diane Joyce,

that, "[b]ut for [Mr. Johnson's] sex, male, he would have been promoted to the position of Road Dispatcher," and that, "[b]ut for Diane Joyce's sex, female, she would not have been appointed to the position. . . ." The Ninth Circuit did not reject these factual findings as clearly erroneous, nor could it have done so on the record before us. We are bound by those findings under Federal Rule of Civil Procedure 52(a).

Societal Attitudes and Discrimination

The most significant proposition of law established by today's decision is that racial or sexual discrimination is permitted under Title VII when it is intended to overcome the effect, not of the employer's own discrimination, but of societal attitudes that have limited the entry of certain races, or of a particular sex, into certain jobs. . . .

In fact, however, today's decision goes well beyond merely allowing racial or sexual discrimination in order to eliminate the effects of prior societal *discrimination*. The majority opinion often uses the phrase "traditionally segregated job category" to describe the evil against which the plan is legitimately (according to the majority) directed. As originally used in *Steelworkers v. Weber* (1979), that phrase described skilled jobs from which employers and unions had systematically and intentionally excluded black workers—traditionally segregated jobs, that is, in the sense of conscious, exclusionary discrimination. But that is assuredly not the sense in which the phrase is used here. It is absurd to think that the nationwide failure of road maintenance crews, for example, to achieve the Agency's ambition of 36.4% female representation is attributable primarily, if even substantially, to systematic exclusion of women eager to shoulder pick and shovel. It is a "traditionally segregated job category" *not* in the *Weber* sense, but in the sense that, because of longstanding social attitudes, it has not been regarded *by women themselves* as desirable work. Or as the majority opinion puts the point, quoting approvingly the Court of Appeals:

> "A plethora of proof is hardly necessary to show that women are generally underrepresented in such positions, and that strong social pressures weigh against their participation."

Given this meaning of the phrase, it is patently false to say that

> [t]he requirement that the "manifest imbalance" relate to a "traditionally segregated job category" provides assurance ... that sex or race will be taken into account in a manner consistent with Title VII's purpose of eliminating the effects of employment discrimination.

There are, of course, those who believe that the social attitudes which cause women themselves to avoid certain jobs and to favor others are as nefarious as conscious, exclusionary discrimination. Whether or not that is so (and there is assuredly no consensus on the point equivalent to our national consensus against intentional discrimination), the two phenomena are certainly distinct. And it is the alteration of social attitudes, rather than the elimination of discrimination, which today's decision approves as justification for state-enforced discrimination. This is an enormous expansion, undertaken without the slightest justification or analysis. . . .

A Requirement of Discrimination

Today's decision does more, however, than merely reaffirm *Weber*, and more than merely extend it to public actors. It is impossible not to be aware that the practical effect of our holding is to accomplish *de facto* [in practice] what the law—in language even plainer than that ignored in *Weber*—forbids anyone from accomplishing *de jure* [by law]: in many contexts, it effectively *requires* employers, public as well as private, to engage in intentional discrimination on the basis of race or sex. This Court's prior interpretations of Title VII, especially the decision in *Griggs v. Duke Power Co.* (1971), subject employers to a potential Title VII suit whenever there is a noticeable imbalance in the representation of minorities or women in the employer's workforce. Even the employer who is confident of ultimately prevailing in such a suit must contemplate the expense and adverse publicity of a trial, because the extent of the imbalance, and the "job relatedness" of his selection criteria, are questions of fact to be explored through rebuttal and counterrebuttal of a *"prima facie* [at first sight] case" consisting of no more than the showing that the employer's selection process "selects those from the protected class at a 'significantly' lesser rate than their counterparts" [B. Schlei & P. Grossman, Employment Discrimination Law 91 (2d ed. 1983)]. If, however, employers are free to discriminate through affirmative action, without fear of "reverse discrimination" suits by their nonminority or male victims, they are offered a threshold defense against Title VII liability premised on numerical disparities. Thus, after today's decision, the *failure* to engage in reverse discrimination is economic folly, and arguably a breach of duty to shareholders or taxpayers, wherever the cost of anticipated Title VII litigation exceeds the cost of hiring less capable (though still minimally capable) workers. (This situation is more likely to obtain, of course, with respect to the least skilled jobs—perversely creating an incentive to discriminate against precisely those members of the nonfavored groups *least* likely to have profited from societal discrimination in the past.) It is predictable, moreover, that this incentive will be greatly magnified by economic pressures brought to bear by government contracting agencies upon employers who refuse to discriminate in the fashion we have now approved. A statute designed to establish a color-blind and gender-blind workplace has thus been converted into a powerful engine of racism and sexism, not merely *permitting* intentional race- and sex-based discrimination, but often making it, through operation of the legal system, practically compelled.

It is unlikely that today's result will be displeasing to politically elected officials, to whom it provides the means of quickly accommodating the demands of organized groups to achieve concrete, numerical improvement in the economic status of particular constituencies. Nor will it displease the world of corporate and governmental employers (many of whom have filed briefs as *amici* [friends of the court] in the present case, all on the side of Santa Clara) for whom the cost of hiring less qualified workers is often substantially less—and infinitely more predictable—than the cost of litigating Title VII cases and of seeking to convince federal agencies by nonnumerical means that no discrimination exists. In fact, the only losers in the process are the Johnsons of the country, for whom Title VII has been not merely repealed, but actually inverted. The irony is that these individuals—predominantly unknown, unaffluent, unorganized—suffer this injustice at the hands of a Court fond of thinking itself the champion of the politically impotent. I dissent.

| "The logic of proportional representa-
tion is now set in concrete."

Brennanism

Daniel Seligman

Daniel Seligman was an editor and columnist at Fortune *magazine from 1950 to 1997.*

The following commentary is from Seligman's Fortune *col-
umn "Keeping Up." Seligman argues that the Supreme Court's
1987 decision in* Johnson v. Transportation Agency, *determining that hiring policies by employers that take account of sex are
constitutionally permissible in certain cases, set in stone the le-
gitimization of affirmative action programs that aim at proportional representation. Seligman contends that the goal of proportional representation in the workforce rests on the faulty logic
that all inequalities in employment must stem from inequalities
in social arrangements, which include employment practices. He
laments the support the* Johnson *decision received from the business community. He believes that the decision wrongly supports
the use of quotas and reverse discrimination to achieve proportional representation.*

Everything about the latest Supreme Court decision on affirmative action—lumpily labeled *Johnson v. Transportation Agency, Santa Clara County, California, et al.* [1987]—
seems totally unastonishing. Possibly this is because all the
principal actors have become so predictable. In the wake of
Johnson, there was the American business community profess-
ing as usual to be delighted with an opinion guaranteeing still

more quotas in employment. The Reagan Administration was as usual looking like a loser. The union of liberal commentators, led by the *New York Times*, was as usual enthusing over the court's murky reasoning. ("On Giving Women a Break" was the smarmy headline atop the *Times*'s editorial.) The Supremes themselves were as usual divided, but the nose count revealed still another majority in the grip of a certain idea.

The Ideal of Proportional Representation

The idea is this: All people are inherently equal in ability and motivation, and so inequalities in employment and income must stem from inequities in our social arrangements. The idea is never stated explicitly in the Court's opinions, and its empirical foundations are rather wobbly; indeed an avalanche of research in biology and psychology has been demonstrating more and more human differences to be innate. Yet the idea continues to sustain Justice Bill Brennan and the Court's other instinctive egalitarians, and it enables them to keep finding that we have a problem needing to be solved any time some ethnic group or sex is "underrepresented" in various jobs. The unstated ideal is proportional representation; The Brennanites' usual way of attaining it is via reverse discrimination.

They have long since made clear that they will not be deterred by the plain language of the law. The Civil Rights Act of 1964 unambiguously states that you cannot require preference "on account of an imbalance which may exist with respect to the total number or percentage of persons of any race ... (or) sex ..." In the 1979 [*Steelworkers v.*] *Weber* case, which is the main ancestor of *Johnson*, Brennan nevertheless upheld a quota plan designed to rectify long-standing imbalances. How did he do it? No sweat: He argued that, sure, the law didn't "require" any such preference, but it "permitted" Kaiser Aluminum to set up preferential plans voluntarily. (In fact, the voluntariness of the plan was a bit of a charade: Kaiser had entered into the plan because its arm was being twisted by federal regulators.) The Court also labored to make *Weber* more palatable by saying that any such plans had to be temporary. This created a difficulty in *Johnson*, because Santa Clara county had labeled its goals "long range." This time Brennan got around the difficulty by arguing that they couldn't really be long range because they envisioned only that the county would "attain" a certain balance (the figure for women was 36.4% of all jobs), not "maintain" it. Pretty smooth, eh?

Not dealt with in Brennan's opinion was another logical difficulty about those goals. In moving mindlessly toward proportional representation, the county had looked around to see who was in the local labor force and then come up with the following goals for minorities: blacks, 1.6%; Hispanics, 14.8%; Asian-Americans, 2.9%; American Indians, 0.4%; handicapped individuals, 6.5%. But unlike the women, who were underrepresented in most job categories, several of these groups were overrepresented. Blacks, for example, were overrepresented in five out of the seven job categories for which the county was hiring. By the logic of the Court's decision, whites should be given preference over blacks in these positions. The American civil rights establishment managed to ignore this awkward fact; both the Urban League and the NAACP [National Association for the Advancement of Colored People] expressed delight with *Johnson*.

The Response of American Businesses

The formal posture of business toward the decision was equally ecstatic. The National Association of Manufacturers, the Business Roundtable, and the Chamber of Commerce were all for *Johnson*, and the press printed encomiums [expressions of praise] to the decision by spokespersons from General Electric, Du Pont, Campbell Soup, Champion International, Eastman Kodak, Philip Morris, and many more. Also weighing in on the side of proportional representation was the American Society for Personnel Administration [ASPA], a kind of trade association for the human resources folk, which filed an amicus curiae [friend of the court] brief that sought to help the court justify group preferences over merit. Laboring to prove that merit isn't all that important, and that it was okay for Santa Clara county to choose a woman over a man who had scored higher on the relevant exam, the ASPA came up with a doctrine that your correspondent had not previously heard of. Said the brief: "It is a standard tenet of personnel administration that there is rarely a single, 'best qualified' person for a job." Somehow one senses that, if the U.S. has a problem with "competitiveness," it is not going to be solved by the personnel department.

Why is American business in this posture? Partly, we assume, because all large corporations now have huge affirmative action bureaucracies representing an insistent internal pressure to support quotas. And partly, we sense, because a lot of C.E.O.s [chief executive officers] have been sold on the doctrine of corporate social responsibility and actually believe they are doing good by enforcing quotas.

The Reagan Administration

The posture of the Reagan Administration is even harder to make sense of. In one case after another, we sit here watching Ron's solicitor general go before the Supreme Court and get clobbered when he tries to make a case against reverse discrimination. The suits in question typically involve large principles but, as in *Johnson*, only a few employees. Meanwhile, Reagan has steadily refused to lift up his fountain pen and, with a stroke thereof, rescind the executive order that now requires all federal contractors to have goals and timetables— and that represents the major source of employment quotas in the U.S. We gather that the President is in this weird position because he just can't bring himself to resolve the dispute between Labor Secretary Bill Brock (who thinks the present system is fine) and Attorney General Ed Meese (who wants to end it). Looking back in dismay, a lot of Reaganites are now telling themselves that the time to have acted decisively against quotas was in the Administration's first few months, when Ron seemed irresistible. They had their chance, and blew it, and the logic of proportional representation is now set in concrete.

> *"Increasing judicial approval for 'reverse' discrimination claims against private-sector employers puts at risk those companies that seek greater diversity."*

The Relevance of *Johnson* for Ad Hoc Affirmative Action Is Unclear

Michael Starr and Adam J. Heft

Michael Starr is partner at Holland & Knight's labor and employment practice in New York City, and Adam J. Heft is an attorney in New York City.

   In the following selection Starr and Heft contend that the relevance of the Supreme Court decision in Johnson v. Transportation Agency *(1987), determining that hiring policies by employers that take account of sex are constitutionally permissible in certain cases, is unclear given several recent lower court decisions that seem to conflict with the* Johnson *decision. Starr and Heft claim that* Johnson *would appear to allow private employers to use sex as a factor in hiring for a position where women are underrepresented. Nonetheless Starr and Heft caution that one recent district court decision in particular appears to have held that such affirmative action is not permitted. The lack of clarity on the issue of ad hoc, or case-by-case, affirmative action, the authors conclude, has left private employers in the dark about the legality of giving preference to qualified woman and minority candidates in hiring decisions.*

Michael Starr and Adam J. Heft, "Ad Hoc Affirmative Action," *National Law Journal*, May 8, 2006. Copyright © 2006 ALM Properties, Inc. Reproduced by permission.

In recent years, employers across all industries have increasingly recognized the value of a diverse work force and engaged in a variety of methods, some more well thought out than others, to attract and retain employees from diverse backgrounds. These efforts are often motivated by the desire to "do the right thing." No one would deny that women and minorities deserve the same opportunities for success as nonminorities and men have had.

But beyond the desire to do good or avoid legal liability for employment discrimination, achieving diversity is also good business. Shareholders and clients are more frequently demanding that an organization's payroll better reflect the make-up of its community. The Equal Employment Opportunity Commission (EEOC) has recognized the link between diversity and corporate achievement, concluding in its report, "Best Practices of Private Sector Employers," that for "the most successful companies . . . pursuing diversity and equal employment opportunity is just as integral a business concept as increasing market share or maximizing profits."

Reverse Discrimination Claims

Unfortunately, attempting to achieve the worthy goal of increasing workplace diversity through ad hoc decisions [decisions made on a case-by-case basis] that advance women or minorities, often made in the absence of, or without strict adherence to, a formal affirmative action plan, can spawn claims of illegal reverse discrimination. Such claims appear to be on the rise. A particularly noteworthy example of this trend is *White v. Alcoa Inc.*, (S.D. Ind. March 27, 2006), where the plaintiff, a white male applicant for a security/paramedic position at an Alcoa plant in Indiana, filed an action alleging that he was passed over in favor of a less qualified female applicant.

In *White*, three male and one female candidates, all of whom had remained in contention after an initial screening, were interviewed and rated by Harold Grossman, the Alcoa employee directing the search, and the four team leaders who worked under him. The interviewers gave a score of 278 points to one male (Anthony Schneider) and 270 to the ultimate plaintiff (Brian White). The one female candidate (Tracee Evans) scored 264 points, and the last male candidate (Oscar Ross) received 259 points. The interviewers then met as a group to formulate final ranking. Evans, who had received the third-highest interview score, was ranked second overall, behind Schneider, but ahead of White.

Before an offer was made, however, Alcoa's human resources department intervened. Having determined that women were underutilized in the job category that encompassed the open position, H.R. representatives told Grossman that if the candidates were all qualified, Alcoa "would have to be seriously looking at" Evans. Grossman balked, insisting that while all four candidates were qualified, Schneider was his first choice. But human resources overruled Grossman and directed him to offer Evans the job. This was ad hoc affirmative action par excellence.

In denying Alcoa's motion for summary judgment, the court rejected as "unconvincing" the interviewers' proffered reasons for not offering White the job—that he did not appear to care whether he received a job offer, and that he might not transition well from his current position—because the human resources manager had essentially ignored the interview process when she directed that the position be offered to Evans. The court said that because the interviewers' preferences were ignored, they could not be relied upon as legitimate reasons to justify Alcoa's decision not to offer White the job. And thus, even though Evans was ranked second and ahead of White before human resources intervened, his claim for sex discrimination, as an unsuccessful male candidate, was sustained.

Preference and Discrimination

The irony of *White*, and of many other "reverse" discrimination cases, is that one man's preference is another man's refusal to discriminate. If Alcoa had selected either of the two men who had "outscored" Evans in the interview, she could have had a viable claim for sex discrimination, perhaps a more viable claim than White's. Given that Grossman had stated that each of the four final candidates was qualified for the open position, that nearly all of the decision-makers were men and that women were underrepresented in the position. Evans would almost certainly have made out a prima facie [at first sight] case for sex discrimination. Nor is it hard to imagine that, notwithstanding her nominally lower score and ranking, Evans might succeed in showing that her gender was at least a "determinative" factor in the decision, which would be enough for her lawsuit to prevail.

Indeed, Evans could also attack the subjective decision-making process itself under the "disparate impact" theory of Title VII of the Civil Rights Act of 1964, arguing that her lower score and ranking reflected covert male bias—a task made easier by the 1991 amendments to Title VII.

Weber and *Johnson*

While public-sector employers are governed by both Title VII and the more exacting standards of the Constitution's equal protection clause, private-sector affirmative action is governed only by Title VII. The standard for that was set by two Supreme Court decisions that seem to have faded into the hoary [ancient] past: *United Steelworkers of America v. Weber* (1979), and *Johnson v. Transportation Agency* (1987). Together, these two cases would seem to hold that a preference for minority (or women) candidates does not transgress anti-discrimination statutes if there was, at the time of the preference, a "manifest imbalance" of minority or female workers in a "traditionally segregated" job category and if the preference did not "unnecessarily trammel" on the interests of nonminority men.

Johnson is particularly relevant, as (like *White*) it concerned the selection of a woman ranked lower than a competing male candidate, whom the trial court had found to be more qualified. Nonetheless, in sustaining the employer's choice, the high court noted that the unsuccessful male candidate "had no absolute entitlement" to the position, but rather that the decision-maker was authorized to promote any one of the candidates who met the eligibility requirements. That is also the situation in *White*, where each of the final candidates was qualified for the position. Writing for the majority in *Johnson*, Justice William J. Brennan addressed this exact point: "It is a standard tenet of personnel administration that there is rarely a single, 'best qualified' person for a job."

Even though Alcoa, a federal contractor, was required to maintain an affirmative action plan—a point ignored by the court—the selection of Evans over the male candidates who scored higher appears to have been an ad hoc decision that went beyond expanding the applicant pool to giving a preference to a woman who, though not less qualified, was not preferred by the predominantly male decision-makers. Under *Weber* and *Johnson*, such a preference does not appear to violate Title VII. Nor is there a requirement that an employer consciously apply a formal affirmative action plan in order for its minority preference to be permissible. This point can clearly be seen in *Johnson*, where the plan's only relevant provision was that decision-makers were authorized to consider a qualified applicant's sex as one factor when selecting for a position within a job classification in which women were traditionally significantly underrepresented.

Employers Seeking Diversity at Risk

Increasing judicial approval for "reverse" discrimination claims against private-sector employers puts at risk those companies that seek greater diversity to achieve what the EEOC called "competitive advantage in the increasingly global economy." If companies like Alcoa are acting improperly by selecting a top-ranking female candidate from a group of four qualified candidates, then it is hard to see when it would ever be acceptable to exercise a preference to correct a "manifest imbalance" of minority or female workers in a "traditionally segregated" job category. If Alcoa had ignored the opportunity to hire a qualified female candidate in a job category in which women were underrepresented, that imbalance would have persisted.

It is a common and justified human resources responsibility to monitor an affirmative action plan, to caution against denying an employment opportunity to a qualified female or minority candidate and to suggest selecting a qualified female or minority candidate for an underrepresented job category. Yet doing so runs the risk of legal liability to the nonselected white male. As with so much in employment law, employers are "damned if you do and damned if you don't," at least until appellate courts give clear approval to ad hoc affirmative action in the private sector.

CHAPTER 4

Validating Limits on Suing Employers for Sex Discrimination

Case Overview

Ledbetter v. Goodyear Tire & Rubber Co. (2007)

In *Ledbetter v. Goodyear Tire & Rubber Co.* the Supreme Court ruled that employees are not able to challenge ongoing pay discrimination if the employer's original discrimination occurred more than 180 days before, even when the employee continues to receive paychecks that are influenced by discrimination. The decision in *Ledbetter* was reversed less than two years later by the passage of the Lilly Ledbetter Fair Pay Act of 2009.

Lilly Ledbetter worked for Goodyear Tire & Rubber Company in Alabama from 1979 until 1998. After her November 1998 retirement she filed suit, asserting a pay discrimination claim under Title VII of the Civil Rights Act of 1964. By the end of 1997 Ledbetter was paid $3,727 per month as an area manager, whereas the lowest-paid male area manager was paid $4,286 per month and the highest-paid male area manager was paid $5,236. Ledbetter claimed that she was paid a discriminatorily low salary because of her sex, and the district court agreed. Upon appeal the court of appeals reversed this decision, determining that she should have filed her claim within 180 days of each discriminatory pay decision and that the clock did not restart with each paycheck. The Supreme Court agreed with the court of appeals.

The five-justice majority claimed that the 180-day limit on filing a sex discrimination claim applies to any disparate treatment based on sex where there is discriminatory intent. Because Ledbetter argued that her paychecks carried forward the discriminatory intent of past decisions, the Court ruled that she should have filed her claim within 180 days of those original decisions. Because the key element of discriminatory intent was missing from the issuance of each paycheck, the Court determined that Ledbetter could not restart the 180-day limit with each paycheck.

The four-justice dissenting opinion disagreed with the majority decision, noting that the common characteristics of pay discrimination are incremental pay differentiation and confidentiality of pay information. The dissent argued that both the pay-setting decision and the actual payment of a discriminatory wage are unlawful practices under Title VII, with each allowing 180 days for filing a claim of pay discrimination.

The Lilly Ledbetter Fair Pay Act of 2009 reversed the *Ledbetter* decision, restoring the position of the U.S. Equal Employment Opportunity Commission (EEOC) prior to *Ledbetter* that pay discrimination on the basis of sex, race, national origin, age, religion, and disability occurs whenever an employee receives a discriminatory paycheck or when a person is otherwise affected by the decision or practice. This amendment to the Civil Rights Act of 1964 thus gives individuals 180 days from the time of each discriminatory paycheck or discriminatory practice to challenge the discrimination.

> "Any unlawful employment practice, in-
> cluding those involving compensation,
> must be presented to the EEOC within
> the period prescribed by statute."

The Court's Decision:
Filing for Pay Discrimination
Is Subject to Time Limits

Samuel A. Alito Jr.

*Samuel A. Alito Jr. was appointed to the U.S. Supreme Court by
President George W. Bush and has served as associate justice
since 2006.*

The following is the majority opinion in the 2007 case of
Ledbetter v. Goodyear Tire & Rubber Co., *wherein the Supreme Court decided that charges of employment discrimination
are time limited according to legislation. Writing for the majority, Alito affirmed a decision of the lower court of appeals that
had determined that Lilly Ledbetter's charge of sex discrimination was unfounded due to a failure to file within the required
period of 180 days from the alleged discrete act of discrimination. In his decision Alito argued that several past cases—or precedents—demand that the Court reject Ledbetter's claim. Although Ledbetter contended that charges of discrimination in
pay are different because of the difficulty in knowing about pay
discrimination, the Court disagreed, concluding that charges of
pay discrimination were subject to the 180-day filing requirement.*

Samuel A. Alito Jr., majority opinion, *Ledbetter v. Goodyear Tire & Rubber Co.*, U.S. Supreme Court, 2007.

This case calls upon us to apply established precedent in a slightly different context. We have previously held that the time for filing a charge of employment discrimination with the Equal Employment Opportunity Commission (EEOC) begins when the discriminatory act occurs. We have explained that this rule applies to any "[d]iscrete ac[t]" of discrimination, including discrimination in "termination, failure to promote, denial of transfer, [and] refusal to hire" [*National Railroad Passenger Corporation v. Morgan* (2002)]. Because a pay-setting decision is a "discrete act," it follows that the period for filing an EEOC charge begins when the act occurs. Petitioner, having abandoned her claim under the Equal Pay Act, asks us to deviate from our prior decisions in order to permit her to assert her claim under Title VII. Petitioner also contends that discrimination in pay is different from other types of employment discrimination and thus should be governed by a different rule. But because a pay-setting decision is a discrete act that occurs at a particular point in time, these arguments must be rejected. We therefore affirm the judgment of the Court of Appeals.

The District Court Decision

Petitioner Lilly Ledbetter (Ledbetter) worked for respondent Goodyear Tire and Rubber Company (Goodyear) at its Gadsden, Alabama, plant from 1979 until 1998. During much of this time, salaried employees at the plant were given or denied raises based on their supervisors' evaluation of their performance. In March 1998, Ledbetter submitted a questionnaire to the EEOC alleging certain acts of sex discrimination, and in July of that year she filed a formal EEOC charge. After taking early retirement in November 1998, Ledbetter commenced this action, in which she asserted, among other claims, a Title VII pay discrimination claim and a claim under the Equal Pay Act of 1963 (EPA).

The District Court granted summary judgment in favor of Goodyear on several of Ledbetter's claims, including her Equal Pay Act claim, but allowed others, including her Title VII pay discrimination claim, to proceed to trial. In support of this latter claim, Ledbetter introduced evidence that during the course of her employment several supervisors had given her poor evaluations because of her sex, that as a result of these evaluations her pay was not increased as much as it would have been if she had been evaluated fairly, and that these past pay decisions continued to affect the amount of her pay throughout her employment. Toward the end of her time with Goodyear, she was being paid significantly less than any of her male colleagues. Goodyear maintained that the evaluations had been nondiscriminatory, but the jury found for Ledbetter and awarded her backpay and damages.

The Court of Appeals' Decision

On appeal, Goodyear contended that Ledbetter's pay discrimination claim was time barred with respect to all pay decisions made prior to September 26, 1997—that is, 180 days before the filing of her EEOC questionnaire. And Goodyear argued that no discriminatory act relating to Ledbetter's pay occurred after that date.

The Court of Appeals for the Eleventh Circuit reversed, holding that a Title VII pay discrimination claim cannot be based on any pay decision that occurred prior to the last pay decision that affected the employee's pay during the EEOC charging period. The Court of Appeals then concluded that there was insufficient evidence to prove that Goodyear had acted with discriminatory intent in making the only two pay decisions that occurred within that time span, namely, a decision made in 1997 to deny Ledbetter a raise and a similar decision made in 1998.

Ledbetter filed a petition for a writ of certiorari [review of the lower court] but did not seek review of the Court of

Appeals' holdings regarding the sufficiency of the evidence in relation to the 1997 and 1998 pay decisions. Rather, she sought review of the following question:

> "Whether and under what circumstances a plaintiff may bring an action under Title VII of the Civil Rights Act of 1964 alleging illegal pay discrimination when the disparate pay is received during the statutory limitations period, but is the result of intentionally discriminatory pay decisions that occurred outside the limitations period."

In light of disagreement among the Courts of Appeals as to the proper application of the limitations period in Title VII disparate-treatment pay cases, we granted certiorari.

Ledbetter's Charge of Discrimination

Title VII of the Civil Rights Act of 1964 makes it an "unlawful employment practice" to discriminate "against any individual with respect to his compensation . . . because of such individual's . . . sex." An individual wishing to challenge an employment practice under this provision must first file a charge with the EEOC. Such a charge must be filed within a specified period (either 180 or 300 days, depending on the State) "after the alleged unlawful employment practice occurred," and if the employee does not submit a timely EEOC charge, the employee may not challenge that practice in court.

In addressing the issue whether an EEOC charge was filed on time, we have stressed the need to identify with care the specific employment practice that is at issue. Ledbetter points to two different employment practices as possible candidates. Primarily, she urges us to focus on the paychecks that were issued to her during the EEOC charging period (the 180-day period preceding the filing of her EEOC questionnaire), each of which, she contends, was a separate act of discrimination. Alternatively, Ledbetter directs us to the 1998 decision denying her a raise, and she argues that this decision was "unlawful because it carried forward intentionally discriminatory disparities from prior years." Both of these arguments fail because they would require us in effect to jettison the defining element of the legal claim on which her Title VII recovery was based.

Ledbetter asserted disparate treatment, the central element of which is discriminatory intent. However, Ledbetter does not assert that the relevant Goodyear decisionmakers acted with actual discriminatory intent either when they issued her checks during the EEOC charging period or when they denied her a raise in 1998. Rather, she argues that the paychecks were unlawful because they would have been larger if she had been evaluated in a nondiscriminatory manner *prior to* the EEOC charging period. Similarly, she maintains that the 1998 decision was unlawful because it "carried forward" the effects of prior, uncharged discrimination decisions. In essence, she suggests that it is sufficient that discriminatory acts that occurred prior to the charging period had continuing effects during that period. This argument is squarely foreclosed by our precedents.

Precedent Set in *Evans*

In *United Air Lines, Inc. v. Evans* (1977), we rejected an argument that is basically the same as Ledbetter's. Evans was forced to resign because the airline refused to employ married flight attendants, but she did not file an EEOC charge regarding her termination. Some years later, the airline rehired her but treated her as a new employee for seniority purposes. Evans then sued, arguing that, while any suit based on the original discrimination was time barred, the airline's refusal to give her credit for her prior service gave "present effect to [its] past illegal act and thereby perpetuate[d] the consequences of forbidden discrimination."

We agreed with Evans that the airline's "seniority system [did] indeed have a continuing impact on her pay and fringe benefits," but we noted that "the critical question [was] whether any present *violation* exist[ed]." We concluded that the continuing effects of the precharging period discrimination did not make out a present violation. As JUSTICE [John Paul] STEVENS wrote for the Court:

> "United was entitled to treat [Evans' termination] as lawful after respondent failed to file a charge of discrimination within the 90 days then allowed by §706(d). A discriminatory act which is not made the basis for a timely charge . . . is merely an unfortunate event in history which has no present legal consequences."

It would be difficult to speak to the point more directly.

The Precedents Set in *Ricks* and *Lorance*

Equally instructive is *Delaware State College v. Ricks* (1980), which concerned a college librarian, Ricks, who alleged that he had been discharged because of race. In March 1974, Ricks was denied tenure, but he was given a final, nonrenewable one-year contract that expired on June 30, 1975. Ricks delayed filing a charge with the EEOC until April 1975, but he argued that the EEOC charging period ran from the date of his actual termination rather than from the date when tenure was denied. In rejecting this argument, we recognized that "one of the *effects* of the denial of tenure," namely, his ultimate termination, "did not occur until later." But because Ricks failed to identify any specific discriminatory act "that continued until, or occurred at the time of, the actual termination of his employment," we held that the EEOC charging period ran from "the time the tenure decision was made and communicated to Ricks."

This same approach dictated the outcome in *Lorance v. AT&T Technologies, Inc.* (1989), which grew out of a change in the way in which seniority was calculated under a collective-bargaining agreement. Before 1979, all employees at the plant in question accrued seniority based simply on years of employment at the plant. In 1979, a new agreement made seniority for workers in the more highly paid (and traditionally male) position of "tester" depend on time spent in that position alone and not in other positions in the plant. Several years later, when female testers were laid off due to low seniority as calculated under the new provision, they filed an EEOC charge alleging that the 1979 scheme had been adopted with discriminatory intent, namely, to protect incumbent male testers when women with substantial plant seniority began to move into the traditionally male tester positions.

We held that the plaintiffs' EEOC charge was not timely because it was not filed within the specified period after the adoption in 1979 of the new seniority rule. We noted that the plaintiffs had not alleged that the new seniority rule treated men and women differently or that the rule had been applied in a discriminatory manner. Rather, their complaint was that the rule was adopted originally with discriminatory intent. And as in *Evans* and *Ricks*, we held that the EEOC charging period ran from the time when the discrete act of alleged intentional discrimination occurred, not from the date when the effects of this practice were felt. We stated:

> "Because the claimed invalidity of the facially nondiscriminatory and neutrally applied tester seniority system is wholly dependent on the alleged illegality of signing the underlying agreement, it is the date of that signing which governs the limitations period."

The EEOC Charging Period

Our most recent decision in this area confirms this understanding. In *Morgan*, we explained that the statutory term "employment practice" generally refers to "a discrete act or single 'occurrence'" that takes place at a particular point in time. We pointed to "termination, failure to promote, denial of transfer, [and] refusal to hire" as examples of such "discrete" acts, and we held that a Title VII plaintiff "can only file a charge to cover discrete acts that 'occurred' within the appropriate time period."

The instruction provided by *Evans, Ricks, Lorance,* and *Morgan* is clear. The EEOC charging period is triggered when a discrete unlawful practice takes place. A new violation does not occur, and a new charging period does not commence, upon the occurrence of subsequent nondiscriminatory acts that entail adverse effects resulting from the past discrimination. But of course, if an employer engages in a series of acts each of which is intentionally discriminatory, then a fresh violation takes place when each act is committed.

Ledbetter's arguments here—that the paychecks that she received during the charging period and the 1998 raise denial each violated Title VII and triggered a new EEOC charging period—cannot be reconciled with *Evans, Ricks, Lorance,* and *Morgan.* Ledbetter, as noted, makes no claim that intentionally discriminatory conduct occurred during the charging period or that discriminatory decisions that occurred prior to that period were not communicated to her. Instead, she argues simply that Goodyear's conduct during the charging period gave present effect to discriminatory conduct outside of that period. But current effects alone cannot breathe life into prior, uncharged discrimination; as we held in *Evans,* such effects in themselves have "no present legal consequences." Ledbetter should have filed an EEOC charge within 180 days after each allegedly discriminatory pay decision was made and communicated to her. She did not do so, and the paychecks that were issued to her during the 180 days prior to the filing of her EEOC charge do not provide a basis for overcoming that prior failure.

The Shifting of Intent

In an effort to circumvent the need to prove discriminatory intent during the charging period, Ledbetter relies on the intent associated with other decisions made by other persons at other times.

Ledbetter's attempt to take the intent associated with the prior pay decisions and shift it to the 1998 pay decision is unsound. It would shift intent from one act (the act that consummates the discriminatory employment practice) to a later act that was not performed with bias or discriminatory motive. The effect of this shift would be to impose liability in the absence of the requisite intent.

Our cases recognize this point. In *Evans*, for example, we did not take the airline's discriminatory intent in 1968, when it discharged the plaintiff because of her sex, and attach that intent to its later act of neutrally applying its seniority rules. Similarly, in *Ricks*, we did not take the discriminatory intent that the college allegedly possessed when it denied Ricks tenure and attach that intent to its subsequent act of terminating his employment when his nonrenewable contract ran out. On the contrary, we held that "the only alleged discrimination occurred—and the filing limitations periods therefore commenced—at the time the tenure decision was made and communicated to Ricks."

The EEOC Filing Deadline

Not only would Ledbetter's argument effectively eliminate the defining element of her disparate-treatment claim, but it would distort Title VII's "integrated, multistep enforcement procedure" [*Occidental Life Ins. Co. of Cal. v. EEOC* (1977)]. We have previously noted the legislative compromises that preceded the enactment of Title VII. Respectful of the legislative process that crafted this scheme we must "give effect to the statute as enacted" [*Mohasco Corp. v. Silver* (1980)], and we have repeatedly rejected suggestions that we extend or truncate Congress' deadlines.

Statutes of limitations serve a policy of repose. They

"represent a pervasive legislative judgment that it is unjust to fail to put the adversary on notice to defend within a specified period of time and that 'the right to be free of stale claims in time comes to prevail over the right to prosecute them'" [*United States v. Kubrick* (1979) (quoting *Railroad Telegraphers v. Railway Express Agency, Inc.*, (1944))].

The EEOC filing deadline "protect[s] employers from the burden of defending claims arising from employment decisions that are long past" [*Ricks*]. Certainly, the 180-day EEOC charging deadline is short by any measure, but "[b]y choosing what are obviously quite short deadlines, Congress clearly intended to encourage the prompt processing of all charges of employment discrimination" [*Mohasco*]. This short deadline reflects Congress' strong preference for the prompt resolution of employment discrimination allegations through voluntary conciliation and cooperation.

An Untimely Claim

A disparate-treatment claim comprises two elements: an employment practice, and discriminatory intent. Nothing in Title VII supports treating the intent element of Ledbetter's claim any differently from the employment practice element. If anything, concerns regarding stale claims weigh more heavily with respect to proof of the intent associated with employment practices than with the practices themselves. For example, in a case such as this in which the plaintiff's claim concerns the denial of raises, the employer's challenged acts (the decisions not to increase the employee's pay at the times in question) will almost always be documented and will typically not even be in dispute. By contrast, the employer's intent is almost always disputed, and evidence relating to intent may fade quickly with time. In most disparate-treatment cases, much if not all of the evidence of intent is circumstantial. Thus, the critical issue in a case involving a long-past performance evaluation will often be whether the evaluation was so far off the mark that a sufficient inference of discriminatory intent can be drawn. This can be a subtle determination, and the passage of time may seriously diminish the ability of the parties and the factfinder to reconstruct what actually happened.

Ledbetter contends that employers would be protected by the equitable doctrine of laches [defense due to delay], but Congress plainly did not think that laches was sufficient in this context. Indeed, Congress took a diametrically different approach, including in Title VII a provision allowing only a few months in most cases to file a charge with the EEOC.

Ultimately, "experience teaches that strict adherence to the procedural requirements specified by the legislature is the best guarantee of evenhanded administration of the law" [*Mohasco*]. By operation of §§2000e-5(e)(1) and 2000e-5(f)(1) a Title VII "claim is time barred if it is not filed within these time limits" [*Morgan*]. We therefore reject the suggestion that an employment practice committed with no improper purpose and no discriminatory intent is rendered unlawful nonetheless because it gives some effect to an intentional discriminatory act that occurred outside the charging period. Ledbetter's claim is, for this reason, untimely. . . .

No Special Treatment for Pay Claims

Ledbetter, finally, makes a variety of policy arguments in favor of giving the alleged victims of pay discrimination more time before they are required to file a charge with the EEOC. Among other things, she claims that pay discrimination is harder to detect than other forms of employment discrimination.

We are not in a position to evaluate Ledbetter's policy arguments, and it is not our prerogative to change the way in which Title VII balances the interests of aggrieved employees against the interest in encouraging the "prompt processing of all charges of employment discrimination" [*Mohasco*] and the interest in repose.

Ledbetter's policy arguments for giving special treatment to pay claims find no support in the statute and are inconsistent with our precedents. We apply the statute as written, and this means that any unlawful employment practice, including those involving compensation, must be presented to the EEOC within the period prescribed by statute.

| "The Court's insistence on immediate contest overlooks common characteristics of pay discrimination."

Dissenting Opinion: Current Pay Disparities Between Men and Women Are Acts of Sex Discrimination

Ruth Bader Ginsburg

Ruth Bader Ginsburg was appointed to the Supreme Court in 1993 by President Bill Clinton. She was the second female justice and the first Jewish woman on the Court.

In the following excerpt from her dissent in the 2007 case of Ledbetter v. Goodyear Tire & Rubber Co., *Justice Ginsburg contends that the Court's decision was mistaken. Ginsburg rejects the Court's determination that pay discrimination consists of a discrete act of discrimination, arguing instead that in many cases pay discrimination is the cumulative effect of multiple acts, referring to precedent in favor of this view. In addition Ginsburg argues that pay discrimination is unique in that salaries are usually concealed, preventing employees from knowing about pay discrimination. Ginsburg believes that Title VII of the Civil Rights Act of 1964 demands that any discrepancy in pay between the sexes can be considered sex discrimination, regardless of how the current discrepancy comes to be.*

Lilly Ledbetter was a supervisor at Goodyear Tire and Rubber's plant in Gadsden, Alabama, from 1979 until her retirement in 1998. For most of those years, she worked as an

Ruth Bader Ginsburg, dissenting opinion, *Ledbetter v. Goodyear Tire & Rubber Co.*, U.S. Supreme Court, 2007.

area manager, a position largely occupied by men. Initially, Ledbetter's salary was in line with the salaries of men performing substantially similar work. Over time, however, her pay slipped in comparison to the pay of male area managers with equal or less seniority. By the end of 1997, Ledbetter was the only woman working as an area manager and the pay discrepancy between Ledbetter and her 15 male counterparts was stark: Ledbetter was paid $3,727 per month; the lowest paid male area manager received $4,286 per month, the highest paid, $5,236.

The Court's Decision

Ledbetter launched charges of discrimination before the Equal Employment Opportunity Commission (EEOC) in March 1998. Her formal administrative complaint specified that, in violation of Title VII, Goodyear paid her a discriminatorily low salary because of her sex. That charge was eventually tried to a jury, which found it "more likely than not that [Goodyear] paid [Ledbetter] a[n] unequal salary because of her sex." In accord with the jury's liability determination, the District Court entered judgment for Ledbetter for backpay and damages, plus counsel fees and costs.

The Court of Appeals for the Eleventh Circuit reversed. Relying on Goodyear's system of annual merit-based raises, the court held that Ledbetter's claim, in relevant part, was time barred. Title VII provides that a charge of discrimination "shall be filed within [180] days after the alleged unlawful employment practice occurred." Ledbetter charged, and proved at trial, that within the 180-day period, her pay was substantially less than the pay of men doing the same work. Further, she introduced evidence sufficient to establish that discrimination against female managers at the Gadsden plant, not performance inadequacies on her part, accounted for the pay differential. That evidence was unavailing, the Eleventh Circuit held, and the Court today [May 29, 2007] agrees, because it was incumbent on Ledbetter to file charges year-by-year, each time Goodyear failed to increase her salary commensurate with the salaries of male peers. Any annual pay decision not contested immediately (within 180 days), the Court affirms, becomes grandfathered, a *fait accompli* [accomplished fact] beyond the province of Title VII ever to repair.

The Uniqueness of Pay Discrimination

The Court's insistence on immediate contest overlooks common characteristics of pay discrimination. Pay disparities often occur, as they did in Ledbetter's case, in small increments; cause to suspect that discrimination is at work develops only over time. Comparative pay information, moreover, is often hidden from the employee's view. Employers may keep under wraps the pay differentials maintained among supervisors, no less the reasons for those differentials. Small initial discrepancies may not be seen as meet for a federal case, particularly when the employee, trying to succeed in a nontraditional environment, is averse to making waves.

Pay disparities are thus significantly different from adverse actions "such as termination, failure to promote, . . . or refusal to hire," all involving fully communicated discrete acts, "easy to identify" as discriminatory. It is only when the disparity becomes apparent and sizable, *e.g.*, through future raises calculated as a percentage of current salaries, that an employee in Ledbetter's situation is likely to comprehend her plight and, therefore, to complain. Her initial readiness to give her employer the benefit of the doubt should not preclude her from later challenging the then current and continuing payment of a wage depressed on account of her sex.

On questions of time under Title VII, we have identified as the critical inquiries: "What constitutes an 'unlawful employment practice' and when has that practice 'occurred'?" Our precedent suggests, and lower courts have overwhelmingly held, that the unlawful practice is the *current payment* of salaries infected by gender-based (or race-based) discrimination—a practice that occurs whenever a paycheck delivers less to a woman than to a similarly situated man.

Two Views of Title VII

Title VII proscribes as an "unlawful employment practice" discrimination "against any individual with respect to his compensation . . . because of such individual's race, color, religion, sex, or national origin." An individual seeking to challenge an employment practice under this proscription must file a charge with the EEOC within 180 days "after the alleged unlawful employment practice occurred."

Ledbetter's petition presents a question important to the sound application of Title VII: What activity qualifies as an unlawful employment practice in cases of discrimination with respect to compensation. One answer identifies the pay-setting decision, and that decision alone, as the unlawful practice. Under this view, each particular salary-setting decision is discrete from prior and subsequent decisions, and must be challenged within 180 days on pain of forfeiture. Another response counts both the pay-setting decision and the actual payment of a discriminatory wage as unlawful practices. Under this approach, each payment of a wage or salary infected by sex-based discrimination constitutes an unlawful employment practice; prior decisions, outside the 180-day charge-filing period, are not themselves actionable, but they are relevant in determining the lawfulness of conduct within the period. The Court adopts the first view, but the second is more faithful to precedent, more in tune with the realities of the workplace, and more respectful of Title VII's remedial purpose.

Discrete Acts and Cumulative Effect

In *Bazemore* [*v. Friday* (1986)], we unanimously held that an employer, the North Carolina Agricultural Extension Service, committed an unlawful employment practice each time it paid black employees less than similarly situated white employees. Before 1965, the Extension Service was divided into two branches: a white branch and a "Negro branch." Employees in the "Negro branch" were paid less than their white counterparts. In response to the Civil Rights Act of 1964, which included Title VII, the State merged the two branches into a single organization, made adjustments to reduce the salary disparity, and began giving annual raises based on nondiscriminatory factors. Nonetheless, "some pre-existing salary disparities continued to linger on." We rejected the Court of Appeals' conclusion that the plaintiffs could not prevail because the lingering disparities were simply a continuing effect of a decision lawfully made prior to the effective date of Title VII. Rather, we reasoned, "[e]ach week's paycheck that delivers less to a black than to a similarly situated white is a wrong actionable under Title VII." Paychecks perpetuating past discrimination, we thus recognized, are actionable not simply because they are "related" to a decision made outside the charge-filing period, but because they discriminate anew each time they issue.

Subsequently, in [*National Railroad Passenger Corporation v.*] *Morgan* [2002], we set apart, for purposes of Title VII's timely filing requirement, unlawful employment actions of two kinds: "discrete acts" that are "easy to identify" as discriminatory, and acts that recur and are cumulative in impact. "[A] [d]iscrete ac[t] such as termination, failure to promote, denial of transfer, or refusal to hire," we explained, "'occur[s]' on the day that it 'happen[s].' A party, therefore, must file a charge within . . . 180 . . . days of the date of the act or lose the ability to recover for it."

"[D]ifferent in kind from discrete acts," we made clear, are "claims . . . based on the cumulative effect of individual acts." The *Morgan* decision placed hostile work environment claims in that category. "Their very nature involves repeated conduct." "The unlawful employment practice" in hostile work environment claims "cannot be said to occur on any particular day. It occurs over a series of days or perhaps years and, in direct contrast to discrete acts, a single act of harassment may not be actionable on its own." The persistence of the discriminatory conduct both indicates that management should have known of its existence and produces a cognizable harm. Because the very nature of the hostile work environment claim involves repeated conduct,

> "[i]t does not matter, for purposes of the statute, that some of the component acts of the hostile work environment fall outside the statutory time period. Provided that an act contributing to the claim occurs within the filing period, the entire time period of the hostile environment may be considered by a court for the purposes of determining liability."

Consequently, although the unlawful conduct began in the past, "a charge may be filed at a later date and still encompass the whole."

Pay disparities, of the kind Ledbetter experienced, have a closer kinship to hostile work environment claims than to charges of a single episode of discrimination. Ledbetter's claim, resembling Morgan's, rested not on one particular paycheck, but on "the cumulative effect of individual acts." She charged insidious discrimination building up slowly but steadily. Initially in line with the salaries of men performing substantially the same work, Ledbetter's salary fell 15 to 40 percent behind her male counterparts only after successive evaluations and percentage-based pay adjustments. Over time, she alleged and proved, the repetition of pay decisions undervaluing her work gave rise to the current discrimination of which she complained. Though component acts fell outside the charge-filing period, with each new paycheck, Goodyear contributed incrementally to the accumulating harm.

Concealed Pay Discrimination

The realities of the workplace reveal why the discrimination with respect to compensation that Ledbetter suffered does not fit within the category of singular discrete acts "easy to iden-tify." A worker knows immediately if she is denied a promo-tion or transfer, if she is fired or refused employment. And promotions, transfers, hirings, and firings are generally public events, known to co-workers. When an employer makes a de-cision of such open and definitive character, an employee can immediately seek out an explanation and evaluate it for pre-text. Compensation disparities, in contrast, are often hidden from sight.

It is not unusual, decisions in point illustrate, for manage-ment to decline to publish employee pay levels, or for employ-ees to keep private their own salaries. Tellingly, as the record in this case bears out, Goodyear kept salaries confidential; em-ployees had only limited access to information regarding their colleagues' earnings.

The problem of concealed pay discrimination is particu-larly acute where the disparity arises not because the female employee is flatly denied a raise but because male counter-parts are given larger raises. Having received a pay increase, the female employee is unlikely to discern at once that she has experienced an adverse employment decision. She may have little reason even to suspect discrimination until a pattern de-velops incrementally and she ultimately becomes aware of the disparity. Even if an employee suspects that the reason for a comparatively low raise is not performance but sex (or an-other protected ground), the amount involved may seem too small, or the employer's intent too ambiguous, to make the is-sue immediately actionable—or winnable.

Further separating pay claims from the discrete employ-ment actions identified in *Morgan*, an employer gains from sex-based pay disparities in a way it does not from a discrimi-natory denial of promotion, hiring, or transfer. When a male employee is selected over a female for a higher level position, someone still gets the promotion and is paid a higher salary; the employer is not enriched. But when a woman is paid less than a similarly situated man, the employer reduces its costs each time the pay differential is implemented. Furthermore, decisions on promotions, like decisions installing seniority systems, often implicate the interests of third-party employees in a way that pay differentials do not. Disparate pay, by contrast, can be remedied at any time solely at the expense of the employer who acts in a discriminatory fashion. . . .

Evidence of Pay Discrimination

To show how far the Court has strayed from interpretation of Title VII with fidelity to the Act's core purpose, I return to the evidence Ledbetter presented at trial. Ledbetter proved to the jury the following: She was a member of a protected class; she performed work substantially equal to work of the dominant class (men); she was compensated less for that work; and the disparity was attributable to gender-based discrimination.

Specifically, Ledbetter's evidence demonstrated that her current pay was discriminatorily low due to a long series of decisions reflecting Goodyear's pervasive discrimination against women managers in general and Ledbetter in particular. Ledbetter's former supervisor, for example, admitted to the jury that Ledbetter's pay, during a particular one-year period, fell below Goodyear's minimum threshold for her position. Although Goodyear claimed the pay disparity was due to poor performance, the supervisor acknowledged that Ledbetter received a "Top Performance Award" in 1996. The jury also heard testimony that another supervisor—who evaluated Ledbetter in 1997 and whose evaluation led to her most recent raise denial—was openly biased against women. And two women who had previously worked as managers at the plant told the jury they had been subject to pervasive discrimination and were paid less than their male counterparts. One was paid less than the men she supervised. Ledbetter herself testified about the discriminatory animus conveyed to her by plant officials. Toward the end of her career, for instance, the plant

149

manager told Ledbetter that the "plant did not need women, that [women] didn't help it, [and] caused problems." After weighing all the evidence, the jury found for Ledbetter, concluding that the pay disparity was due to intentional discrimination.

The Court's Interpretation of Title VII

Yet, under the Court's decision, the discrimination Ledbetter proved is not redressable under Title VII. Each and every pay decision she did not immediately challenge wiped the slate clean. Consideration may not be given to the cumulative effect of a series of decisions that, together, set her pay well below that of every male area manager. Knowingly carrying past pay discrimination forward must be treated as lawful conduct. Ledbetter may not be compensated for the lower pay she was in fact receiving when she complained to the EEOC. Nor, were she still employed by Goodyear, could she gain, on the proof she presented at trial, injunctive relief requiring, prospectively, her receipt of the same compensation men receive for substantially similar work. The Court's approbation of these consequences is totally at odds with the robust protection against workplace discrimination Congress intended Title VII to secure.

This is not the first time the Court has ordered a cramped interpretation of Title VII, incompatible with the statute's broad remedial purpose. Once again, the ball is in Congress' court. As in 1991, the Legislature may act to correct this Court's parsimonious reading of Title VII [accomplished by the passage of the Lilly Ledbetter Fair Pay Act of 2009].

| "Alito had the better of the argument as to congressional language and the Court's own precedents."

Ledbetter Was Not Unjustly Decided

Stuart Taylor Jr.

Stuart Taylor Jr. is a senior fellow in governance studies at the Brookings Institution, a contributing editor at Newsweek, *and a regular columnist for* National Journal.

In the following selection Taylor argues that despite the media hype to the contrary, Ledbetter v. Goodyear Tire & Rubber Co. *(2007) was correctly decided. Taylor contends that the language of Title VII of the Civil Rights Act of 1964 clearly sets a statute of limitations of 180 days. The facts of the case and Supreme Court precedents, or past decisions, clearly lead to the conclusion that Ledbetter did not have a valid case of sex discrimination, according to Taylor. Taylor also critiques the jury's decision in Ledbetter's original case that decided in her favor, later overturned by both the federal appeals court and the Supreme Court.*

This headline ["Injustice 5, Justice 4"], borrowed from a *New York Times* editorial, pretty well sums up the news media's portrayal of a May 29 Supreme Court ruling that an Alabama woman suing her former employer for sex-based pay discrimination had not filed her claim within the congressionally prescribed time limit.

In *The Times*, that headline could only refer to one grouping: The usual four conservatives plus sometime-conservative

Stuart Taylor Jr., "Injustice 5, Justice 4," *National Journal*, vol. 39, no. 23, June 9, 2007, pp. 17–18. Reproduced by permission.

151

Justice Anthony Kennedy voting down the usual four liberals. With Bush-appointed Justice Samuel Alito writing the majority opinion, and Clinton-appointed Justice Ruth Bader Ginsburg reading her dissent from the bench and urging Congress to "correct" the Court, this rather technical case, *Ledbetter v. Goodyear Tire & Rubber*, instantly became a magnet for media moaning of the barbarians-at-the-gate genre.

"The Supreme Court struck a blow for discrimination this week," *The Times* began. The Court "has read the law so rigidly that it has misread life," chimed in the *Los Angeles Times*. *The Washington Post*'s front-page news report devoted (by my count) four paragraphs to the nuts and bolts of the decision, four and a half paragraphs to the majority's analysis and supportive quotes, and 17 and a half paragraphs to Ginsburg, her dissent, and other critics. "A harsh and rigid reading of the law . . . striking for its lack of empathy," Ellis Cose complained in *Newsweek*. He seconded the American Civil Liberties Union's charge that this was an "astonishing decision" by an "activist court."

Are Alito and company really such heartless, pro-discrimination brutes? Hardly. Ginsburg's dissent was well put. But Alito had the better of the argument as to congressional language and the Court's own precedents, in my view. And as a policy matter, it's far from clear that justice would be better served by the Ginsburg approach of opening the door wide to employees who, like the plaintiff in this case, wait for many years to claim long-ago—and thus difficult to disprove—pay discrimination.

The majority's reading of the relevant provisions of Title VII of the 1964 Civil Rights Act, which bans employment discrimination based on (among other things) sex, rested on three points that Ginsburg did not dispute.

- Congress provided an unusually short statute of limitations for Title VII lawsuits such as plaintiff Lilly Ledbetter's—180 days "after the alleged employment practice occurred"—in a political compromise designed to promote conciliation over litigation.

• Title VII required Ledbetter to prove that the "employment practice" involved intentional discrimination in pay based on sex.

• Her employer, Goodyear Tire & Rubber, did not *intentionally* discriminate against her during the 180 days before she filed her complaint.

Case closed, one might think: This lawsuit was time-barred *by Congress.*

But lawyers for Ledbetter, who was paid significantly less than any of her male colleagues, and Justice Ginsburg had a theory to get around the 1964 act's seemingly plain language:

Because supervisors intentionally discriminated against Ledbetter by putting her on a lower-paid track than her male colleagues years before she filed her claim, the argument goes, then—*even if nobody ever intentionally discriminated against her again*—each new paycheck amounted to a new act of discrimination, resetting the 180-day clock.

That's a stretch. True, most federal appeals courts have reached similar conclusions, but never, as Alito stressed, has the Supreme Court allowed such a Title VII suit to proceed without evidence that at least some intentional discrimination occurred within the 180-day period.

Four of the Court's prior decisions—in 1977, 1980, 1989, and 2002—held that Title VII's statute of limitations cut off any claims based on discriminatory acts that occurred more than 180 days before the claim was filed, even if those acts continued to adversely affect the plaintiff's pay or status into the 180-day period.

Ginsburg stressed another decision, *Bazemore v. Friday,* from 1986. But while somewhat ambiguous, *Bazemore* involved allegations of intentional, race-based pay discrimination during, as well as before, the 180-day period.

The *Ledbetter* case exemplifies the policy judgment underlying such congressionally mandated time limits. The main acts of discrimination alleged by Ledbetter dated to the early 1980s and mid-1990s, when she says a supervisor retaliated against her for shunning his sexual advances by giving her smaller raises than similarly situated men. Ledbetter knew no later than 1992 that she was earning less than most male colleagues. But she waited to sue until July 1998, when she was ready to retire. By the time of trial, the alleged harasser had died, leaving Goodyear in no position to dispute her claims.

The approach proposed by Ginsburg and the three other dissenters could effectively nullify Congress's 180-day statute of limitations in all, or at least most, pay-discrimination lawsuits—even, Alito suggested, if the plaintiff waits 20 years to sue after learning of a single allegedly discriminatory act. Ginsburg responded that judges could use legal doctrines including "laches" to throw out claims filed unreasonably late. Or, as Alito explained, they might not.

The inevitable cost of any statute of limitations is that some valid claims will be time-barred. Congress, not the courts, is supposed to strike the cost-benefit balance. And Congress is free to change or fine-tune the provision to make it more plaintiff-friendly, as Ginsburg and others have urged. But is it the Court's job to fine-tune it by strained interpretation?

Meanwhile, the suggestions by Ginsburg and the media that the decision leaves women such as Ledbetter with no adequate remedy for pay discrimination—because they may not even know what their male peers are paid until more than 180 days after the allegedly discriminatory pay-setting decision—are vastly exaggerated.

It's true that *some* victims of pay discrimination will be initially ignorant of their peers' pay and thus out of luck as far as Title VII is concerned. But Ledbetter, who waited six or more years to sue after learning of the pay disparities, is not one of them.

Besides, Title VII is not the only remedy for sex-based pay discrimination. The Equal Pay Act of 1963 requires employers to pay women as much as men doing "equal work" in the same establishment, with exceptions including merit pay. This law does not require proof of intentional discrimination. And it has a much longer, three-year statute of limitations.

Ledbetter sued under the Equal Pay Act as well as under Title VII. But the trial judge threw out the former claim. The exact reasons are unclear, but it appears that few men at Goodyear had jobs similar enough to Ledbetter's to meet the definition of "equal work." Ledbetter did not appeal, perhaps because the big bucks are in punitive damages, which are unavailable under the Equal Pay Act.

The judge allowed the Title VII claim to go to trial. The jury found sex-based pay discrimination and awarded Ledbetter $223,776 in back pay, $4,662 for mental anguish—and $3,285,979 in punitive damages. The judge reduced this to $60,000 in back pay and the congressional maximum $300,000 in (mostly punitive) damages.

This is the award that the justices overturned (as had a federal appeals court) on the ground that the Title VII claim should never have gone to the jury because there was no proof of intentional discrimination during the 180-day period set by Congress.

By the way, it's debatable, if legally irrelevant, whether the jury was right to find that Ledbetter was a victim of sex discrimination. While she and two other women testified that male supervisors at the plant were openly biased against women, other witnesses disagreed. And the evidence as to Goodyear's intent was old and stale.

It was clearly established, on the other hand, that the pay disparities between Ledbetter and similarly situated men were largely attributable to the cumulative effect of repeated layoffs, which made her ineligible for raises in 1986, 1987, 1988, and 1990, and which she has not alleged to be discriminatory.

Beyond that, before the case went to the jury, a federal magistrate judge found that Ledbetter's relatively low pay reflected "weak" job performance, not sex discrimination. He noted that most of her performance evaluations were "at or near the bottom": 15th out of 16 area managers, and 23rd out of 24 salaried employees in tire assembly in both 1996 and 1997, for example. Ledbetter said the evaluations were tainted by discrimination.

Ginsburg, whose dissents from this and other 5-4 conservative rulings have brought much media adulation, has said she feels "lonely" on the bench since Justice Sandra Day O'Connor, her only female colleague, retired. And some suggest that O'Connor would have voted with Ginsburg in this case.

Perhaps. But a 2002 decision relaxing Title VII's filing deadline in a case involving a years-long pattern of racial harassment suggests otherwise. The majority opinion, then described by *The New York Times* as "an important victory for workers," was written by Justice Clarence Thomas, whom Adam Cohen of *The Times* maligned after the *Ledbetter* decision for "reflexively" opposing "discrimination claims of minorities and women." The author of the dissent, which called for strict enforcement of the statute of limitations against "all types of Title VII" plaintiffs, was Sandra Day O'Connor.

> *"The* Ledbetter *decision tells employers that as long as they can hide their discriminatory behavior for six months, they've got the green light to treat female employees badly forever."*

Congress Should Overturn *Ledbetter*

Dahlia Lithwick

Dahlia Lithwick is a contributing editor at Newsweek *and senior editor and legal correspondent at* Slate.

In the following article Lithwick argues that the Ledbetter v. Goodyear Tire & Rubber Co. *(2007) decision needs to be overturned by an act of Congress. Doing this, she claims, would reinstate the original reading of Title VII, allowing women such as Lilly Ledbetter to bring charges of pay discrimination when they find out about discriminatory pay within 180 days of a discriminatory paycheck, regardless of when the discriminatory pay started. Lithwick strongly disapproves of the efforts by some members of Congress to block a law reinstating this original reading, suggesting that such efforts treat women disparagingly.*

On Wednesday, [April 23, 2008,] Senate Republicans blocked a bill that would have overturned a Supreme Court ruling that sharply limited pay-discrimination suits based on gender under Title VII [the bill was ultimately passed and enacted in 2009]. In *Ledbetter v. Goodyear* (2007), the Supreme Court, by a 5-4 margin, held that the clock for the stat-

Dahlia Lithwick, "How Dumb Are We? How Long Will Women Shoulder the Blame for the Pay Gap?" *Slate*, April 26, 2008. Copyright © 2008 Washingtonpost. Newsweek Interactive Co. LLC. Reproduced by permission.

ute of limitations on wage discrimination begins running when the employer first makes the decision to discriminate, and does not run for all the subsequent months—or in this case, years—that the disparate paychecks are mailed. Justice Samuel Alito, writing for the court, found that the plaintiff in this case, Lilly Ledbetter, was time-barred from filing her discrimination suit because it took more than 180 days after she first got stiffed to discover that she was being stiffed on account of her gender. The court agreed her jury verdict should be overturned.

Protecting Women

Many of the Republicans who blocked the vote to reinstate the original reading of Title VII claimed they were doing so to protect women—read "stupid women"—from the greedy clutches of unprincipled plaintiffs' attorneys and from women's own stupid inclination to sit around for years—decades even—while being screwed over financially before they bring suit. That means they were, in effect, just protecting us from the dangerous laws that protect us. Whew.

For the purely Vulcan [the Roman god of fire] reading of the case, Justice Alito's opinion offers some good reading. But for those of you who suspect that gender discrimination rarely comes amid the blaring of French horns and accompanied by an engraved announcement that you are being screwed over, it's worth having a gander at Justice Ruth Bader Ginsburg's dissent.

Ledbetter's Case

Ledbetter worked for Goodyear Tire in Atlanta for almost 20 years. When she retired, she was, according to Ginsburg, "the only woman working as an area manager and the pay discrepancy between Ledbetter and her 15 male counterparts was stark: Ledbetter was paid $3,727 per month; the lowest paid male area manager received $4,286 per month, the highest paid, $5,236." So she filed a suit under Title VII, and a jury awarded her more than $3 million in damages. The jury found it "more likely than not that [Goodyear] paid [Ledbetter] a[n] unequal salary because of her sex." You see, Ledbetter hadn't just negotiated herself some lame salary. She was expressly barred by her employer from discussing her salary with her co-workers who were racking up raises and bonuses she didn't even know about. She found out about the disparity between her pay and her male colleagues' earnings only because someone finally left her an anonymous tip.

There is plenty of evidence that all this had nothing to do with her job performance. Quoting Ginsburg again, "Ledbetter's former supervisor, for example, admitted to the jury that Ledbetter's pay, during a particular one-year period, fell below Goodyear's minimum threshold for her position." The jury also heard evidence that "another supervisor—who evaluated Ledbetter in 1997 and whose evaluation led to her most recent raise denial—was openly biased against women" and that "two women who had previously worked as managers at the plant told the jury they had been subject to pervasive discrimination and were paid less than their male counterparts. One was paid less than the men she supervised." Ledbetter was told directly by the plant manager that the "plant did not need women, that [women] didn't help it, [and] caused problems."

Stop me when you're convinced that maybe her gender was the issue here . . .

A Proposed Law

The Lilly Ledbetter Fair Pay Act [of 2007], already passed by the House [July 31, 2007], would have reinstated the law as it was interpreted by most appellate courts and the Equal Employment Opportunity Commission, i.e., that every single discriminatory paycheck represents a new act of discrimination and that the 180-day period begins anew with every one. Yet

42 members of the Senate—including Majority Leader Harry Reid, but only procedurally to keep the bill alive—voted to block cloture. How can that be? As Kia Franklin notes here: Women in the United States are paid only 77 cents for every dollar earned by men; African-American women earn only 63 cents, and Latinas earn only 52 cents for every dollar paid to white men. Yet the *Ledbetter* decision tells employers that as long as they can hide their discriminatory behavior for six months, they've got the green light to treat female employees badly forever. Why isn't this problem sufficiently real to be addressed by Congress?

Have a look at some of the reasons proffered:

The White House [under President George W. Bush] threatened to veto the bill even if Congress passed it. Why? The measure would "impede justice and undermine the important goal of having allegations of discrimination expeditiously resolved." Of course, there is a place for finality in the law, and nobody wants businesses to face prospective lawsuits for conduct from 20 years earlier. But unless an employee is psychic, 180 days is simply not long enough to sniff out an ongoing pattern of often-subtle pay discrimination. The notion that expeditiousness in resolving legal disputes should altogether trump one's ability to prove them is cynical beyond imagining. And the very notion that extending the statute of limitations somehow encourages scads of stupid women to loll around accepting unfair wages for decades in the hopes of hitting the litigation jackpot in their mid-70s is just insulting. "Sorry, kids! SpaghettiOs again tonight, but just you wait till 2037! We'll dine like kings, my babies!"

Sen. Orrin Hatch, R-Utah, did one better in insulting women when he said, "The only ones who will see an increase in pay are some of the trial lawyers who bring the cases." See, now this is the argument that holds that the same women who are too stupid to bring timely discrimination claims are also too stupid to avoid being manipulated by those scheming plaintiffs' attorneys. First off, some of us still believe that those damn civil rights attorneys do good things. But what really galls me here is the endless, elitist recitation that it's only the really dumb people—you know, the injured, the sick, and the women—who aren't smart enough to avoid being conned by them into filing frivolous lawsuits.

Here's the other reason proffered to oppose the equal-pay bill: According to the invaluable [online news site] Firedoglake, it seems that some women themselves are actually to blame for their inability to negotiate. No need to fix Title VII! Just build more aggressive women! Women also are apparently to blame for not chatting with their male colleagues about the differences in their wages, even when that's explicitly forbidden, as it was in Ledbetter's case. So remember, ladies, it's better to be fired for discussing your wages than to be paid less for being a woman.

All of which brings us to Sen. John McCain, R-Ariz., who skipped the vote on equal pay altogether because he was out campaigning [in the 2008 presidential race]. (Hillary Clinton and Barack Obama both showed up to support it.) McCain's opposition to the bill was expressed thusly: He's familiar with the pay disparity but believes there are better ways to help women find better-paying jobs. "They need the education and training, particularly since more and more women are heads of their households, as much or more than anybody else." As my colleague Meghan O'Rourke pointed yesterday [April 25, 2008], all that is code for the obtuse claim that the fact that women earn 77 cents on the dollar *for the same work as men* will somehow be fixed by more training for women as opposed to less discrimination by men. Wow. Hey! We should develop the superpowers of heat vision and flight, as well.

The Need to Change Congress

So, 42 members of the U.S. Senate blocked a bill that would allow victims of gender discrimination to learn of and prove discrimination in those rare cases in which their employers don't cheerfully discuss it with them at the office Christmas party. And the reasons for blocking it include the fact that women are not smart enough to file timely lawsuits, not smart enough to avoid being manipulated by vile plaintiffs' lawyers, not smart enough to know when they are being stiffed, and—per John McCain—not well-trained enough in the first place to merit equal pay.

So how dumb are we? Well, if we don't vote some people who actually respect women into Congress soon, we just may be as dumb as those senators think.

> *"The Lilly Ledbetter Fair Pay Act would open the door to a flood of lawsuits, some frivolous, that employers would find difficult or impossible to defend against, no matter their ultimate merit."*

The Lilly Ledbetter Fair Pay Act Will Create Many Problems

Andrew M. Grossman

Andrew M. Grossman is senior legal policy analyst in the Center for Legal and Judicial Studies at The Heritage Foundation.

In the following selection Grossman contends that many negative consequences will follow passage of the Lilly Ledbetter Fair Pay Act, enacted after he wrote this piece. Grossman argues that there are at least five purposes to statutes of limitations of the sort that prevented Ledbetter from having a successful sex discrimination charge: freshness of evidence, resolving discrimination quickly, preventing strategic behavior by plaintiffs, encouraging efficiency, and promoting certainty and stability. Grossman claims that by eliminating narrow interpretation of the 180-day statute of limitations in Ledbetter v. Goodyear Tire & Rubber Co. *(2007), the act will open up the door to a large number of frivolous claims, encouraging employers to make decisions that may end up harming the women the act is supposed to help.*

Andrew M. Grossman, "The Ledbetter Act: Sacrificing Justice for 'Fair' Pay," *Heritage Foundation Legal Memorandum #34*, January 7, 2009. Reproduced by permission.

Congressional leaders have said that they will fast-track the Lilly Ledbetter Fair Pay Act, a bill that would allow pay discrimination lawsuits to proceed years or even decades after alleged discrimination took place. [The bill quickly passed in the House and Senate and was signed into law by President Barack Obama on January 29, 2009.] Proponents say that the legislation is necessary to overturn a Supreme Court decision that misconstrued the law and impaired statutory protections against discrimination, but the Court's decision reflected both longstanding precedent and Congress's intentions at the time the law was passed.

Several Concerns About the Act

In addition, eliminating the limitations period on claims would be bad policy. Since ancient Roman times, all Western legal systems have featured statutes of limitations for most legal claims. Indeed, they are so essential to the functioning of justice that U.S. courts will presume that Congress intended a limitations period and borrow one from an analogous law when a statute is silent. While limitations periods inevitably cut off some otherwise meritorious claims, they further justice by blocking suits where defensive evidence is likely to be stale or expired, prevent bad actors from continuing to harm the plaintiff and other potential victims, prevent gaming of the system (such as destroying defensive evidence or running up damages), and promote the resolution of claims. By eliminating the time limit on lawsuits, the Ledbetter Act would sacrifice these benefits to hand a major victory to trial lawyers seeking big damage payoffs in stale suits that cannot be defended.

The Ledbetter Act would also lead to myriad unintended consequences. Foremost, it would push down both wages and employment, as businesses change their operations to avoid lawsuits. Perversely, it could actually put women, minorities, and workers who are vocal about their rights at a disadvantage if employers attempt to reduce legal risk by hiring fewer individuals likely to file suit against them or terminating those already in their employ.

Rather than effectively eliminate Title VII's limitations period, Congress could take more modest, less risky steps to ease the law's restrictions, if such change is warranted. Most directly, it could lengthen the limitations period to two or three years to match the periods in similar laws. Another option is to augment the current limitations period with a carefully drafted "discovery rule" so that the time limit on suing begins running only when an employee reasonably suspects, or should reasonably suspect, that he or she has been discriminated against. While either of these options would sacrifice some of the benefits of the current limitations period, they are far superior alternatives to throwing the law wide open to stale claims and abuse.

The Ledbetter Suit

For all the rhetoric about the Supreme Court's *Ledbetter* [*v. Goodyear Tire & Rubber Co.* (2007)] decision—the *New York Times*, for one, called it "a blow for discrimination"—it addresses not the substance of gender discrimination but the procedure that must be followed to assert a pay discrimination claim. Specifically, the case presented only the question of when a plaintiff may file a charge alleging pay discrimination with the Equal Employment Opportunity Commission (EEOC), a prerequisite to suing.

Lilly Ledbetter, who worked for Goodyear Tire and Rubber Co. from 1979 until 1998 as a factory supervisor, filed a formal EEOC charge in July 1998 and then a lawsuit in November, the same month that she retired. Her claim was that after she rebuffed the advances of a department foreman in the early 1980s, he had given her poor performance evaluations, resulting in smaller raises than she otherwise would have earned, and that these pay decisions, acting as a baseline, continued to affect the amount of her pay throughout her employment. She said she had been aware of the pay disparity since at least 1992.

Initially, Ledbetter sued under the Equal Pay Act of 1963 (EPA) and Title VII of the Civil Rights Act of 1964, a more general anti-discrimination statute. The EPA, unlike Title VII, has been interpreted not to require proof that pay discrimination was intentional but just that an employer paid an employee less for equal work without a good reason for doing so. For such claims, the EPA imposes a two-year statute of limitations, meaning that an employee can collect deficient pay from any discriminatory pay decisions made during that period, whether or not the employer intended to discriminate in any of those decisions. Title VII, while imposing a shorter filing deadline of 180 days and requiring proof of intent to discriminate, allows for punitive damages, which the EPA does not. Perhaps for this reason, Ledbetter abandoned her EPA claim after the trial court granted summary judgment on it in favor of her former employer.

On her Title VII claim, however, Ledbetter prevailed at trial before a jury, which awarded her $223,776 in back pay, $4,662 for mental anguish, and a staggering $3,285,979 in punitive damages. The judge reduced this total award to $360,000, plus attorneys' fees and court costs.

Appeal to the Supreme Court

Goodyear appealed, and the Eleventh Circuit Court of Appeals reversed the decision on the grounds that Ledbetter had not provided sufficient evidence to prove that an intentionally discriminatory pay decision had been made within 180 days of her EEOC charge. Ledbetter appealed to the Supreme Court, challenging not that determination but only the Court of Appeals' application of Title VII's limitations period.

In a decision by Justice Samuel Alito, the Supreme Court held that the statute's requirement that an EEOC charge be brought within 180 days of an "alleged unlawful employment practice" precluded Ledbetter's suit, because her recent pay raises were not intentionally discriminatory. Ledbetter argued that the continuing pay disparity had the effect of shifting intent from the initial discriminatory practice to later pay decisions, performed without bias or discriminatory motive. The Court, however, had rejected this reasoning in a string of prior decisions standing for the principle that a "new violation does not occur, and a new charging period does not commence, upon the occurrence of subsequent nondiscriminatory acts that entail adverse effects resulting from the past discrimination." For those familiar with the law, this appeared to be a rehash of a 1977 case that reached the same conclusion on identical grounds.

Thus, the Court affirmed the lower decision against Ledbetter.

The Purposes of Limitations Periods

That result did not speak to the merits of Ledbetter's case—that is, whether she had suffered unlawful discrimination years before—but only to the application of the statute's limitations period. Although it seems intrinsically unfair to many that a legal technicality should close the courthouse doors, statutes of limitations, as the majority of the Court observed, do serve several essential functions in the operation of law that justify their cost in terms of barred meritorious claims. In general, limitations periods serve five broad purposes.

Justice [Joseph] Story best articulated the most common rationale for the statute of limitations: "It is a wise and beneficial law, not designed merely to raise a presumption of payment of a just debt, from lapse of time, but to afford security against stale demands, after the true state of the transaction may have been forgotten, or be incapable of explanation, by reason of the death or removal of witnesses" [*Bell v. Morrison* (1828)].

Indeed, *Ledbetter* itself illustrates this function. Different treatment, such as pay disparities, may be easy to prove even after much time has lapsed, because the kinds of facts at issue are often documented and, indeed, are rarely in dispute. More contentious, however, is the defendant's discriminatory intent, which Title VII requires in addition to proof of disparate treatment. The evidence proving intent can be subtle—for example, "whether a long-past performance evaluation . . . was so far off the mark that a sufficient inference of discriminatory intent can be drawn." With the passage of time, witnesses' memories may fade, stripping their accounts of the details necessary to resolve the claim. Evidence may be lost or discarded. Indeed, witnesses may disappear or perish—the supervisor whom Ledbetter accused of misconduct had died by the time of trial. Sorting out the subtleties of human relationships a decade or more in the past may be an impossible task for parties and the courts, one at which the defendant, who did not instigate the suit, will be at a particular disadvantage. This seems to have been the case in *Ledbetter*.

Statutes of limitations, in contrast, require a plaintiff to bring his or her claim earlier, when evidence is still fresh and the defendant has a fair chance of mustering it to mount a defense. In this way, statutes of limitations also serve to prevent fraudulent claims whose veracity cannot be checked due to passage of time.

Promoting Good and Preventing Strategic Behavior

Second, statutes of limitations also help to effectuate the purposes of law. They encourage plaintiffs to diligently prosecute their claims, thereby achieving the law's remedial purpose. This is particularly the case for statutes such as those forbidding discrimination in employment practices, where Congress has created causes of action to supplement government enforcement actions. Litigation under such statutes is, in part, a public good, because the plaintiff in a meritorious suit secures justice not just for himself but for similarly situated victims, as well as the public at large, which has expressed its values through the law. Anti-discrimination law is the archetypical example of an area where private suits can promote far broader good. Other victims and the public are best served when workers who believe they have been subject to discrimination have the incentive to investigate the possible unlawful conduct, document it, and then challenge it in a timely fashion. This was an explicit goal of the Civil Rights Act of 1964, whose drafters reasoned that the short limitations period and mandatory EEOC administrative process would lead most discrimination complaints to be resolved quickly, through cooperation and voluntary compliance.

Third, time limits on filing lawsuits prevent strategic behavior by plaintiffs. In some cases, plaintiffs may wait for evidence favorable to the defense to disappear or be discarded, for memories to fade and witnesses to move on, before bringing claims. Particularly under laws that allow damages continuing violations or punitive damages, plaintiffs may face the incentive to keep quiet about violations as the potential pool of damages grows. Concerns that plaintiffs will game the system in this way are so prevalent that an entire doctrine of judge-created law, known as "laches," exists to combat certain of these abuses. Laches, however, is applied inconsistently, and courts often decline its exercise in enforcing statutory rights. A limitations period puts a limit on the extent to which plaintiffs can game the law by delaying suit.

Efficiency and Stability

Fourth, time-limiting the right to sue furthers efficiency. Valuable claims are likely to be investigated and prosecuted promptly, while most of dubious merit or value are "allowed to remain neglected." Thus, "the lapse of years without any attempt to enforce a demand creates, therefore, a presumption against its original validity, or that it has ceased to subsist" [*Weber v. Bd. of Harbor Comm'rs* (1873)]. Statutes of limitations, then, are one way that our justice system focuses its limited resources on the most valuable cases, maximizing its contribution to the public good.

Finally, there is an intrinsic value to repose. It promotes certainty and stability. Putting a deadline on claims protects a business's or individual's settled expectations, such as accounting statements or income. At some point, surprises from the past, in the form of lawsuits, cease to be possible. As with adverse possession of land, the law recognizes that, though a wrong may have been done, over time certainty of rights gains value.

For these important reasons, statutes of limitation are ubiquitous in the law and have been since ancient Roman times. Limitations periods necessarily close the courthouse doors to some potentially worthwhile claims—an outcome so harsh that it would be "pure evil," observed Oliver Wendell Holmes, if it were not so essential to the operation of law. That a single good claim has been barred, then, proves not that the deadline for suit is unfair or unwise but only that justice cannot provide a remedy in every case.

The Ledbetter Act

Nonetheless, editorial reaction to *Ledbetter* was swift and almost entirely negative, with most writers drawing from Justice [Ruth Bader] Ginsburg's bombastic dissent (which she read in part from the bench) calling the majority's reasoning "cramped" and "incompatible with the statute's broad purpose." Ginsburg's logic, repeated on the opinion pages, and often news pages, of countless newspapers, was that Ledbetter was a member of a protected class (women), performed work equal to that of the dominant class (men), and was compensated less for that work due to gender-based discrimination. End of story. Pay discrimination, Ginsburg argued, is different than other forms of discrimination and is more akin to a "hostile work environment" claim, which by its nature involves repeated, ongoing conduct. But this is creative reimagining of the statute: Nowhere in it is there any room for the limitations period present in the statute or indeed any of the other requirements that Congress crafted.

Unfortunately, though, it was Ginsburg's dissent, and her unseemly urging that "once again, the ball is in Congress' court," that spurred the drafters of the Lilly Ledbetter Fair Pay Act, which was introduced soon after the Court issued its decision and passed the House in short order. The bill would adopt Ginsburg's view, amending a variety of anti-discrimination laws to the effect that a violation occurs "each time wages, benefits, or other compensation is paid" that is affected by any discriminatory practice. In this way, the law would simply eliminate the limitations period as applied to many cases.

Under the Ledbetter Act, employees could sue at any time after alleged discrimination occurred, so long as they have received any compensation affected by it in the preceding 180 days. While this would certainly reverse *Ledbetter*, it goes much further by removing any time limitation on suing in pay-related cases, even limitations relating to the employee's learning of the discrimination—an approach that is known in other contexts, such as fraud, as a "discovery rule." This new rule is also broader in that it would apply to any (alleged) discrimination that has had an (alleged) effect on pay, such as an adverse promotion decision. In addition, retirees could bring suits alleging pay-related discrimination that occurred decades ago if they are presently receiving benefits, such as pensions or health care, arguably effected by the long-ago discrimination.

Dangers of the Act

In these ways, the Ledbetter Act would allow cases asserting extremely tenuous links between alleged discrimination and differences in pay, which may result from any number of non-discriminatory factors, such as experience. Employers would be forced to defend cases where plaintiffs present evidence of a present wage gap, allegations of long-ago discrimination, and a story connecting the two. As wage differences between employees performing similar functions are rampant—consider how many factors may be relevant to making a wage determination—a flood of cases alleging past discrimination resulting in present disparity would likely follow passage. In addition to investigatory and legal expenses, employers will face the risk of punitive damages and the difficulty of rebutting assertions of discriminatory acts from years or decades ago.

The flood of lawsuits would not be endless, however, because, as Eric Posner observes, employers can be expected to change their hiring, firing, and wage practices to reduce the risk of lawsuits. To the extent that disparities in treatment are the result of discrimination, this may undercut its effects. But if, as Posner puts it, businesses "start paying workers the same amount even though their productivity differs because they fear that judges and juries will not be able to understand how productivity is determined," the law would impose significant costs on businesses and, by extension, consumers and the economy. The result would be a hit to employment and wages, combined with higher prices for many goods and services.

Perversely, the Ledbetter Act may actually harm those it is intended to protect. In making employment decisions, businesses would consider the potential legal risks of hiring women, minorities, and others who might later bring lawsuits against them and, as a result, hire fewer of these individuals. Even though this discrimination would violate the law, it would be difficult for rejected applicants to prove. Other employers might simply fire employees protected by Title VII— and especially those who are vocal about their rights under the law—to put a cap on their legal liabilities. Again, this would be illegal, but difficult to prove.

These kind of unintended consequences have been a chief effect of the Americans with Disabilities Act, which prohibits discrimination against individuals with disabilities and enforces that prohibition through civil lawsuits. Today, the disabled earn less and work far less than they did prior to enactment of the ADA, and a number of economists, including MIT's Daron Acemoglu, blame the ADA for reducing the number of employment opportunities available to the disabled. In this way, by dramatically increasing employers' exposure to potential liability when they hire members of protected classes, the Ledbetter Act would put members of those classes at a disadvantage in the labor marketplace. . . .

Far beyond reversing the result of a single Supreme Court decision—one that, viewed fairly, was consistent with precedent and fairly represented Congress's intentions—the Lilly Ledbetter Fair Pay Act would open the door to a flood of lawsuits, some frivolous, that employers would find difficult or impossible to defend against, no matter their ultimate merit. Rather than help employees, the bill could end up hurting them by reducing wages and job opportunities—at a time when unemployment is rising and many are nervous about their job prospects. Instead, Congress should recognize that statutes of limitations serve many important and legitimate purposes and reject proposals that would allow litigants to evade them.

Organizations to Contact

The editors have compiled the following list of organizations concerned with the issues debated in this book. The descriptions are derived from materials provided by the organizations. All have publications or information available for interested readers. The list was compiled on the date of publication of the present volume; the information provided here may change. Be aware that many organizations take several weeks or longer to respond to inquiries, so allow as much time as possible.

American Civil Liberties Union (ACLU)
125 Broad St., 18th Floor, New York, NY   10004
(212) 549-2500
e-mail: infoaclu@aclu.org
Web site: www.aclu.org

The American Civil Liberties Union (ACLU) is a national organization that works to defend the rights guaranteed by the U.S. Constitution. Its primary work is to support court cases against government actions that violate these rights. The ACLU publishes and distributes numerous policy statements and reports, including "Venus and Mars in Separate Classrooms?"

Cato Institute
1000 Massachusetts Ave. NW, Washington, DC   20001-5403
(202) 842-0200 • fax: (202) 842-3490
Web site: www.cato.org

The Cato Institute is a public policy research foundation dedicated to limiting the role of government, protecting individual liberties, and promoting free markets. The institute commissions a variety of publications, including books, monographs, briefing papers, and other studies. Among its publications are the quarterly magazine *Regulation*, the bimonthly *Cato Policy Report*, and articles such as "Liberal Academics Get What They Ask For."

Concerned Women for America (CWA)
1015 Fifteenth St. NW, Suite 1100, Washington, DC   20005
(202) 488-7000 • fax: (202) 488-0806
Web site: www.cwfa.org

Concerned Women for America (CWA) is a public policy women's organization that has the goal of bringing biblical principles into all levels of public policy. CWA focuses on promoting biblical values on six core issues—family, sanctity of human life, education, pornography, religious liberty, and national sovereignty—through prayer, education, and social influence. The organization offers brochures, fact sheets, and articles on its Web site.

Equal Rights Advocates (ERA)
1663 Mission St., Suite 250, San Francisco, CA   94103
(415) 621-0672 • fax: (415) 621-6744
e-mail: info@equalrights.org
Web site: www.equalrights.org

Equal Rights Advocates (ERA) works to protect and secure equal rights and economic opportunities for women and girls. The organization also fights for women's equality through litigation and advocacy. ERA produces several publications covering issues of equal opportunity, respectful and safe treatment, and work and family balance, including the *Know Your Rights* brochure entitled "Sex Discrimination."

Human Rights Campaign (HRC)
1640 Rhode Island Ave. NW, Washington, DC   20036-3278
(202) 628-4160 • fax: (202) 347-5323
e-mail: hrc@hrc.org
Web site: www.hrc.org

The Human Rights Campaign (HRC) is America's largest civil rights organization working to achieve gay, lesbian, bisexual, and transgender (GLBT) equality. HRC works to secure equal rights for GLBT individuals at the federal and state levels by lobbying elected officials and mobilizing grassroots supporters. Among the organization's publications is the report *Transgender Inclusion in the Workplace.*

Lambda Legal
120 Wall St., Suite 1500, New York, NY   10005-3904
(212) 809-8585 • fax: (212) 809-0055
e-mail: members@lambdalegal.org
Web site: www.lambdalegal.org

Lambda Legal is a legal organization working for the civil rights of lesbians, gay men, and people with HIV/AIDS. The organization works toward this goal by pursuing impact litigation, education, and advocacy to make the case for equality in state and federal court, in the Supreme Court, and in the court of public opinion. Among the many publications the organization produces is the article titled "Transgender People in the Workplace."

Leadership Conference on Civil and Human Rights
1629 K St. NW, 10th Floor, Washington, DC   20006
(202) 466-3311
Web site: www.civilrights.org

The Leadership Conference on Civil and Human Rights (the Leadership Conference) is a coalition of more than two hundred national human rights organizations. Its mission is to promote the enactment and enforcement of effective civil rights legislation and policy. The organization's Web site features numerous fact sheets and other publications, including "Key Supreme Court Cases for Civil Rights."

Legal Momentum
395 Hudson St., New York, NY   10014
(212) 925-6635 • fax: (212) 226-1066
e-mail: policy@legalmomentum.org
Web site: www.legalmomentum.org

Legal Momentum is a legal defense and education fund dedicated to advancing the rights of women and girls through litigation and public policy advocacy. Among the publications available from Legal Momentum is the report *From the Ground Up: Building Opportunities for Women in Construction.*

National Coalition for Men (NCFM)

932 C St., Suite B, San Diego, CA 92101
(619) 231-1909
e-mail: ncfm@ncfm.org
Web site: www.ncfm.org

The National Coalition for Men (NCFM) is a nonprofit educational organization committed to ending sex discrimination. NCFM works to raise awareness about the ways sex discrimination affects men and boys. Among the publications available at NCFM's Web site is the article "Men's Reproductive Rights."

National Organization for Women (NOW)

1100 H St. NW, 3rd Floor, Washington, DC 20005
(202) 628-8669 • fax: (202) 785-8576
Web site: www.now.org

The National Organization for Women (NOW) is the largest organization of feminist activists in the United States working to take action to bring about equality for all women. NOW works to eliminate discrimination and harassment in the workplace, schools, the justice system, and all other sectors of society; to secure abortion, birth control, and reproductive rights for all women; to end all forms of violence against women; to eradicate racism, sexism, and homophobia; and to promote equality and justice. NOW has many publications available at its Web site, including the fact sheet "Women Deserve Equal Pay."

For Further Research

Books

Howard Ball, *The Supreme Court in the Intimate Lives of Americans: Birth, Sex, Marriage, Childrearing, and Death.* New York: New York University Press, 2002.

Barbara J. Berg, *Sexism in America: Alive, Well, and Ruining Our Future.* Chicago: Lawrence Hill Books, 2009.

Robert H. Bork, *The Tempting of America: The Political Seduction of the Law.* New York: Simon & Schuster, 1991.

Warren Farrell, *The Myth of Male Power: Why Men Are the Disposable Sex.* Lanham, MD: Simon & Schuster, 1993.

Barry Friedman, *The Will of the People: How Public Opinion Has Influenced the Supreme Court and Shaped the Meaning of the Constitution.* New York: Farrar, Straus and Giroux, 2009.

David J. Garrow, *Liberty and Sexuality: The Right to Privacy and the Making of* Roe v. Wade. New York: Macmillan, 1994.

Mark R. Levin, *Men in Black: How the Supreme Court Is Destroying America.* Washington, DC: Regnery Publishing, 2005.

Linda C. McClain and Joanna L. Grossman, eds., *Gender Equality: Dimensions of Women's Equal Citizenship.* New York: Cambridge University Press, 2009.

Sandra Day O'Connor, *The Majesty of the Law: Reflections of a Supreme Court Justice.* New York: Random House, 2003.

Gerald N. Rosenberg, *The Hollow Hope: Can Courts Bring About Social Change?* 2nd ed. Chicago: University of Chicago Press, 2008.

Jay Sekulow, *Witnessing Their Faith: Religious Influence on Supreme Court Justices and Their Opinions.* New York: Rowman & Littlefield, 2006.

Jeffrey Toobin, *The Nine: Inside the Secret World of the Supreme Court.* New York: Anchor Books, 2008.

Melvin I. Urofsky, *Affirmative Action on Trial: Sex Discrimination in* Johnson v. Santa Clara. Lawrence: University Press of Kansas, 1997.

Lee Walzer, *Marriage on Trial: A Handbook with Cases, Laws, and Documents.* Santa Barbara, CA: ABC-CLIO Press, 2005.

Joan Williams, *Unbending Gender: Why Family and Work Conflict and What to Do About It.* New York: Oxford University Press, 2000.

Bob Woodward and Scott Armstrong, *The Brethren: Inside the Supreme Court.* New York: Simon and Schuster, 1979.

Periodicals (by case)

Frontiero v. Richardson (1973):

Kari Balog, "Equal Protection for Homosexuals: Why the Immutability Argument Is Necessary and How It Is Met," *Cleveland State Law Review*, vol. 53, 2005–06.

Cris Carmody, "Judge Ginsburg's Ex-clients Reflect Upon Their Cases; The 'Widows Benefits' Plaintiff Recalls How She Urged Him to Sue," *National Law Journal*, June 28, 1993.

David Cole, "Strategies of Difference: Litigating for Women's Rights in a Man's World," *Law & Inequality: A Journal of Theory and Practice*, February 1984.

Donna Meredith Matthews, "Avoiding Gender Equality," *Women's Rights Law Reporter*, Winter 1998.

Tony Mauro, "Paternity Ward," *American Lawyer*, February 2001.

Betsy B. McKenny, *"Frontiero v. Richardson*: Characterization of Sex-Based Classifications," *Columbia Human Rights Law Review*, Fall-Winter 1974.

Linda Strite Murnane, "Legal Impediments to Service: Women in the Military and the Rule of Law," *Duke Journal of Gender Law & Policy*, May 2007.

Orr v. Orr (1979):

Tresa Baldas, "States Challenge Traditional Alimony," *National Law Journal*, February 11, 2008.

John L. Capell III and Clinton B. Smith, brief of appellant, *Orr v. Orr*, U.S. Supreme Court, 1979.

Emmanuel E. Edem, "Alimony for Men: The Thrust of Recent Decisions of the Supreme Court of the United States," *Oklahoma City University Law Review*, Summer 1981.

Andy Ho, "Why Men Should Not Be Entitled to Alimony," *Malaysian Insider*, June 22, 2009.

W.F. Horsley, brief of appellee, *Orr v. Orr*, U.S. Supreme Court, 1979.

Jennifer L. McCoy, "Spousal Support Disorder: An Overview of Problems in Current Alimony Law," *Florida State University Law Review*, Winter 2005.

Diane M. Signoracci, "A Husband's Constitutional Right Not to Pay Alimony," *Ohio State Law Journal*, Winter 1980.

Johnson v. Transportation Agency (1987):

Roger Clegg, "Faculty Hiring Preferences and the Law," *Chronicle of Higher Education*, May 19, 2006.

Louis Fischer, "Voluntary Gender-Conscious Affirmative Action Plans: The Supreme Court Decision in *Johnson v. Transportation Agency*," *Equity & Excellence in Education*, Spring 1987.

Michael L. Foreman, "Hire the Rainbow," *Legal Times*, April 19, 2004.

Jyotin Hamid, "Diversity Rationale and Private Sector Affirmative Action Policies," *Labor & Employment Law*, Winter 2009.

William L. Kandel, "Johnson v. Transportation Agency: A Revival for Affirmative Action," *Employee Relations Law Journal*, Summer 1987.

Peter Kirsanow, "Patton & Preferences: Diversity Plans Are Vulnerable," *National Review Online*, February 9, 2004. www.nationalreview.com.

Paul Craig Roberts and Lawrence M. Stratton Jr., "Color Code," *National Review*, March 20, 1995.

Martha S. West, "History Lessons," *Women's Review of Books*, February 1996.

Ledbetter v. Goodyear Tire & Rubber Co. (2007):

Ryan J. Fleming, "Pregnancy Discrimination Revived?" *Legal Intelligencer*, June 12, 2009.

Richard Thompson Ford, "Bad Think," *Slate*, May 30, 2007.

Adam L. Grundvig, "*Ledbetter v. Goodyear*: The U.S. Supreme Court Rubs Salt in Plaintiff's Disparate Pay Title VII Wounds," *Journal of Law & Family Studies*, vol. 10, no. 1, 2007.

Stephanie Mencimer, "Courting Disaster," *Mother Jones*, February 7, 2008.

New York Times, "Injustice 5, Justice 4," May 31, 2007.

Katha Pollitt, "Tough Luck, Ladies," *The Nation*, June 7, 2007.

Phyllis Schlafly, "Barack's Bailout for Trial Lawyers," *Townhall.com*, January 13, 2009.

Gerald Skoning, "Overruled by Legislation: Conservative Court and Democratic Congress Is a Toxic Combo for Employers," *National Law Journal*, October 5, 2009.

Karen Lee Torre, "Lilly Ledbetter Is No Victim," *Connecticut Law Tribune*, January 12, 2009.

Index